PIONEERS OF THE
AEROPLANE

USBORNE PUBLISHING

Acknowledgements
Key to picture positions:
(T) top, (C) centre, (B) bottom,
(L) left, (R) right.

British Airways: 44(BR)

Gibbs-Smith, Charles: 6, 7, 8(B),
9, 13(TL), 16(TL), 18, 19,
20(BR), 22(T)(C), 23(C),
27(TR)(CR), 28, 29(CL)(CR)(B),
30(C)(B), 31(C), 32(B), 33(B),
34(T), 36(BR), 37, 38(B), 40(T)

Keystone: 38(TL)

Mansell Collection: 32(C)(CR),
39(T)

National Portrait Gallery, London:
8(T)

Popperfoto: 29(C)(B) portraits,
39(B)

Radio Times Hulton Picture Library:
31(B), 32(CL), 39(C)

Science Museum, London: 11(C)
(B), 25(BL)(BR), 33(C), 36(BL)

Illustrators

Peter Griffin, D. Harley, Peter
Henville, John Hoffer, Trevor
Holder, Tony Joyce, R. A.
Sherrington, Michael Strand,
John Thompson, Mike Tregenza
and John Walsh.

Editor
Ray Kingsley

Picture Research
Millicent Trowbridge

Art Director
John Strange

First published in 1975 by
Usborne Publishing Ltd
20 Garrick Street
London WC2

© Text: Charles Gibbs-Smith, 1975
© Artwork: Usborne Publishing Ltd,
1975

Made and printed in England by
Hazell Watson & Viney Ltd,
Aylesbury, Bucks

ISBN 0 86020 012 4

PIONEERS OF THE
AEROPLANE
C H GIBBS-SMITH

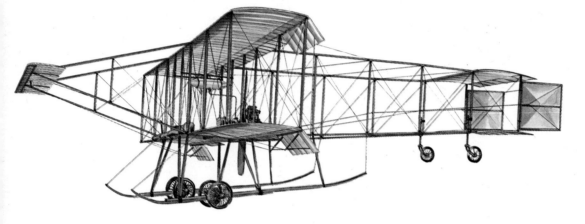

CONTENTS

4	Flight in Nature
6	Man in the Air
8	The Father of Aeronautics
11	The Visionary Designers
12	The Helicopter Craze
14	The First Take-Off
16	Man Learns to Fly
18	The Camera and the Aviator
20	Gliders and the Box-Kite
22	Control in the Air
24	The First Powered Flight
26	The First Practical Aeroplane
28	Europe Learns to Fly
30	The First Monoplanes
32	Wilbur in Europe
34	Flying the Wright A
36	Orville in America
38	Across the English Channel
40	The Champagne Airshow
42	Appendix 1; 1910-1930
44	Appendix 2; Then and Now
46	A Time Chart of Aviation 'Firsts'
47	Index

Flight in Nature

Nature has evolved a large number of flying machines, chiefly birds, bats and insects. These creatures inspired the desire to fly in man, but it was only in the 19th Century that man began to understand how birds fly. Only then could inventors begin to design flying machines that were heavier than air.

▶ A bat's wings are made of smooth membranes stretched behind stiff spars formed by their 'arms'. Early aircraft designers frequently copied this type of structure.

Most of the thrust which carries a bird forwards through the air is produced by these primary feathers.

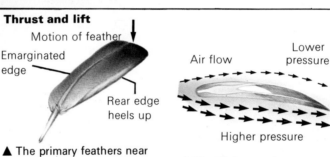

Thrust and lift

Motion of feather

Emarginated edge

Rear edge heels up

Air flow

Lower pressure

Higher pressure

How a bird flies

▼ A bird in flight moves its wings as shown in the strip sequence below. Until men understood that the lift for bird flight comes from the inner parts of the wing, and the thrust from the outer parts, they could not produce a successful flying machine. Most of the forward thrust comes from the propeller action of the primary feathers during the downstroke.

▲ The primary feathers near the ends of a bird's wing are 'emarginated'. This means that there is more feather surface behind the quill than in front. When these feathers are beaten downwards, they twist and push the air backwards much like a propeller and produce *thrust*.

▲ The lift for bird flight comes from the flow of air across the inner parts of the wings. Air pressure is lower above the wing than below because the air has to travel farther across the curved top surface. The result is an upward suction or *lift*.

Nature's helicopter

▶ The hummingbird can hover while feeding off flowers. For hovering flight, the bird rears up its body and continues to flap its wings as in level flight. When the angle of the body becomes so steep, the movement of the wings produces thrust upwards like a helicopter. If the bird wishes to draw back from the flower, it can swivel its wings at the shoulders and produce thrust rearwards and upwards. Then it can lean its body forward again to fly away horizontally.

The down-stroke

As the wings are pulled downwards, the primary feathers at the wing tips spread and twist to an angle with the rest of the wing. The primaries force the air backwards much like the propeller of an aeroplane, and the thrust pushes the wings forwards.

◀ The gannet spends much of its time in gliding flight, with its wings rigidly outstretched. Gliding flight proved to be the best model for manned flying machines. The rigid wing was much more easily imitated than the complex motion of the flapping wing.

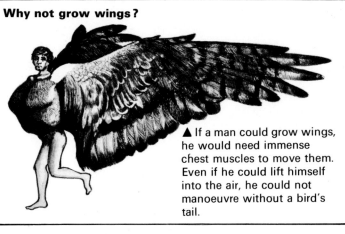
◀ This pigeon is raising its wings for a strong down-stroke as part of a quick take-off. Note the open tail. Opening, closing and swivelling its tail lets the bird manoeuvre in the air far better than any aeroplane.

Backstroke

Thrust
Wing motion
Wing motion
Wing angle
Wing angle
Wing tilts backwards

Forward stroke

Wing angle
Wing tilts forwards

Bird Flight and Flying Machines

The sight of birds in flight drove ancient man to dream of human flight and to imagine winged angels and other holy flying creatures. But apart from supplying the inspiration for man's desire to fly, the bird was a bad model for a heavier-than-air flying machine that could carry a man. The bird has a very light structure and exceedingly powerful muscles with which to flap its wings. A man, on the other hand, is heavy-boned and has comparatively weak muscles.

Sir George Cayley was the first to understand that man must model his flying machines on the *gliding* bird, with wings rigidly outstretched. He saw the need for propelling an aircraft forwards by some other means than flapping wings, so that the wings could be used for lift alone.

The great Otto Lilienthal began his career as an aviator by studying bird flight. He followed Cayley in realising that a bird is pushed through the air by the propeller action of its primary feathers.

The Wright brothers learned a valuable lesson from watching the flight of buzzards. The Wrights copied the way those soaring birds twisted the tips of their wings to keep their balance in the air. This led them to develop the first complete system of flight control. They then went on to make the world's first powered flights and the first practical aeroplane.

The up-stroke
As the wings are moved upwards, the primary feathers separate slightly to allow the air to slip through. At the top of the stroke, they are opened again to prepare for the next down-stroke.

Man in the Air

Since early history, man's dream of imitating the flight of birds has driven him to experiment with a variety of flying machines. From time to time, bold and foolhardy 'pioneers' have fixed wings to themselves and plunged off hills or high buildings in attempts to fly. They had little success and often maimed or killed themselves.

A number of devices with aeronautical features have been used throughout history. These include the arrow with its stabilising feathers, the boomerang, the kite and the windmill. The kite is really an aeroplane without an engine, and the windmill a passive propeller turned by the wind.

Toy makers in the Middle Ages soon reversed the working of the windmill and made models of actively rotating windmill sails which soared into the sky. These were the ancestors of the aircraft propeller. In simple terms, the principles of the kite and the windmill were combined in the propeller-driven aeroplane.

The great artist and scientist Leonardo da Vinci was the first fine mind to try to solve the problems of flight. Most of his work dealt with ornithopters — flapping-wing aircraft based on bird or bat flight. Leonardo's machines would never have flown because he wrongly believed that a bird beats its wings downwards and backwards. Unfortunately, his designs were not published until the late 19th Century, so he did not inspire other early scientists to continue his work.

Many streams of scientific progress had to come together before a manned aeroplane could fly under its own power. Aerodynamics — the forces acting on a flying body — had to be understood. Structures had to be studied and successful flying models built. A lightweight power unit — the petrol engine — was necessary, and this in turn had to wait until petroleum products were widely available. Good propellers had to be developed which could throw enough air backwards to push an aircraft forwards. Finally, a system of flight controls had to be invented from glider experiments before pilots could trust themselves to the air in powered machines.

All of these streams came together at the right moment in Wilbur and Orville Wright. After perfecting the glider, the Wright brothers built and flew the first successful powered aeroplanes in 1903, 1904 and 1905. Their achievements sparked the world of inventors to go ahead and conquer the air and all the problems of navigating it. Six years after the first successful flight, the aeroplane was a practical method of transport, and several types of machine could be bought and flown reliably.

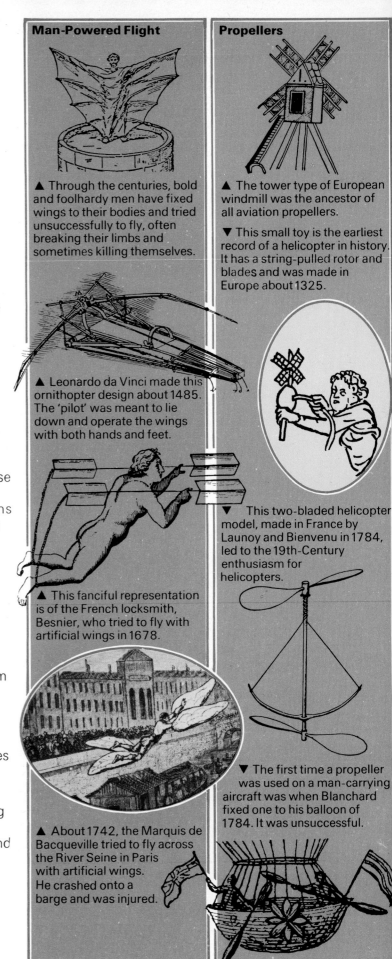

Man-Powered Flight

▲ Through the centuries, bold and foolhardy men have fixed wings to their bodies and tried unsuccessfully to fly, often breaking their limbs and sometimes killing themselves.

▲ Leonardo da Vinci made this ornithopter design about 1485. The 'pilot' was meant to lie down and operate the wings with both hands and feet.

▲ This fanciful representation is of the French locksmith, Besnier, who tried to fly with artificial wings in 1678.

▲ About 1742, the Marquis de Bacqueville tried to fly across the River Seine in Paris with artificial wings. He crashed onto a barge and was injured.

Propellers

▲ The tower type of European windmill was the ancestor of all aviation propellers.

▼ This small toy is the earliest record of a helicopter in history. It has a string-pulled rotor and blades and was made in Europe about 1325.

▼ This two-bladed helicopter model, made in France by Launoy and Bienvenu in 1784, led to the 19th-Century enthusiasm for helicopters.

▼ The first time a propeller was used on a man-carrying aircraft was when Blanchard fixed one to his balloon of 1784. It was unsuccessful.

Kites

▲ Some of the earliest kites in Europe were dragon-shaped with wings, which would have been much larger than shown here. This type disappeared after the 16th Century.

▲ The plane surface kite in a diamond form was first seen in Europe in the early 17th Century and became the standard type for many years. This is the earliest known illustration (1618).

▲ This is one of the earliest illustrations of a kite in Europe, published in an English book in 1634. It clearly shows the stabilising tail.

Parachutes

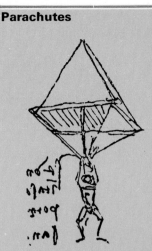

▲ The earliest design for a parachute was drawn by Leonardo da Vinci about 1485. Leonardo probably made a model of this parachute.

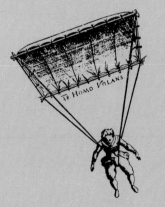

▲ Another early idea for a parachute, probably never tried, was drawn by Veranzio about 1595. It is based on a ship's sail held by four poles.

▲ The first successful man-carrying parachute was made and used by the Frenchman Garnerin in 1797. It was folded like an umbrella, carried up under a balloon, and then cut free.

Balloons

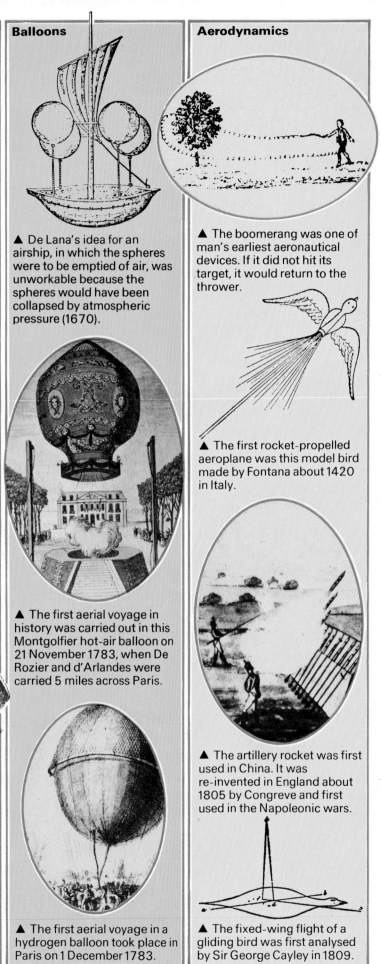

▲ De Lana's idea for an airship, in which the spheres were to be emptied of air, was unworkable because the spheres would have been collapsed by atmospheric pressure (1670).

▲ The first aerial voyage in history was carried out in this Montgolfier hot-air balloon on 21 November 1783, when De Rozier and d'Arlandes were carried 5 miles across Paris.

▲ The first aerial voyage in a hydrogen balloon took place in Paris on 1 December 1783.

Aerodynamics

▲ The boomerang was one of man's earliest aeronautical devices. If it did not hit its target, it would return to the thrower.

▲ The first rocket-propelled aeroplane was this model bird made by Fontana about 1420 in Italy.

▲ The artillery rocket was first used in China. It was re-invented in England about 1805 by Congreve and first used in the Napoleonic wars.

▲ The fixed-wing flight of a gliding bird was first analysed by Sir George Cayley in 1809.

The Father of Aeronautics

▼ In 1849, after a lifetime of aeroplane experiments, Cayley built this full-scale triplane. The machine was equipped with flappers to be operated by the pilot. The flappers were intended for propulsion only and not for producing lift. The machine was tested with a boy on board. Cayley wrote of the experiment. "A boy of about ten years of age was floated off the ground for several yards on descending a hill, and also for about the same space by persons pulling the apparatus against a very slight breeze by a rope."

Sir George Cayley (1773–1857) was an English baronet and a wealthy landowner who lived at Brompton Hall in Yorkshire. Cayley laid the foundations of the science of aerodynamics. He wrote about and experimented with flying models and full-scale aircraft, and also designed two remarkable airships.

The upper fin and tailplane were fixed but adjustable.

This movable rudder and elevator could be controlled by the pilot by means of a tiller inside the fuselage.

This three-wheel undercarriage used Cayley's light-weight cycle-type tension wheels.

▶ The whirling arm had been used earlier for testing cannon balls and windmill sails, but Cayley was the first man to build one for testing aeroplane wings. The arm was made to whirl by dropping a weight on the end of the cord. Small aeroplane wings could be fixed on the arm at varying angles for testing lift and drag.

▶ Cayley heard about or saw a toy helicopter made in France and made his own version in 1796. Its blades were feathers stuck into corks, and it was operated by a bow-drill mechanism. It was a drawing of this toy, published by Cayley in 1809, which led directly to the widespread helicopter experiments in the 19th Century and to the modern helicopter.

The triplane wings were designed to provide a sturdy structure. Wing surfaces were stretched cloth which curved into shape in flight. Wing area was 338 square feet. Total empty weight was 130 pounds.

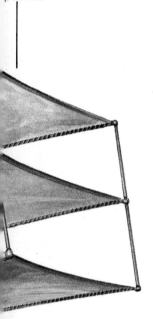

The pilot was supposed to operate these flappers to propel the glider. On this flight, the flappers were fixed, and the boy was only a passenger

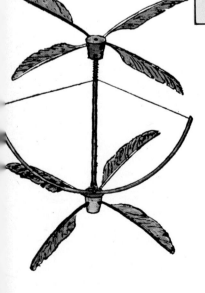

Sir George Cayley

Sir George Cayley was one of the greatest aeronautical pioneers in history. He was the true inventor of the modern type of aeroplane, with its fixed wings and movable surfaces for flight control.

Cayley's basic work in aerodynamics — the study of motion in the air — was published in 1809–10. He then went on to design and build several sophisticated flying machines. In 1853, he sent his coachman off in a free-flying glide at Brompton Hall near Scarborough. The controls were fixed, but this was the first true glider flight in history. Altogether, Cayley was responsible for some 24 new inventions in aviation.

Before Cayley, men concentrated on designing ornithopters, which had flapping wings in imitation of birds. Cayley saw that this was foolish and would lead nowhere. He realised that if men were to fly, they would have to take the rigidly held wings of the gliding or soaring bird as their example, and then provide either propellers or propulsive flappers as an external method of propulsion.

Cayley also wrote about his inventions and his theories, and these writings were reprinted and influenced every inventor who came after. The biplane. for example, can be traced to Cayley's triplane idea that Stringfellow used in his 1868 model.

Apart from his life-long interest in flying, Cayley was also an outstanding inventor in other fields. His inventions included the hot-air engine, which was in world-wide use in industry for over a century; the modern cycle-type wheel; and the caterpillar tractor, from which all present-day tracked vehicles and tanks are descended. When one of his workmen lost a hand in an accident, Cayley invented an excellent artificial hand to replace it. He was also an expert on land drainage and railway safety devices. Cayley remained almost unknown to the world at large for nearly a century, but he is now universally acclaimed as the man who inspired the world to fly.

▼ This remarkable glider design, with rear stabilising and control surfaces and a car on cycle-type wheels, was published by Cayley in 1852. If proper attention had been paid to this drawing, there could have been controllable man-carrying gliders by the 1860's.

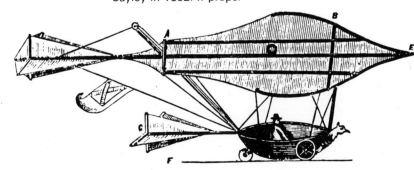

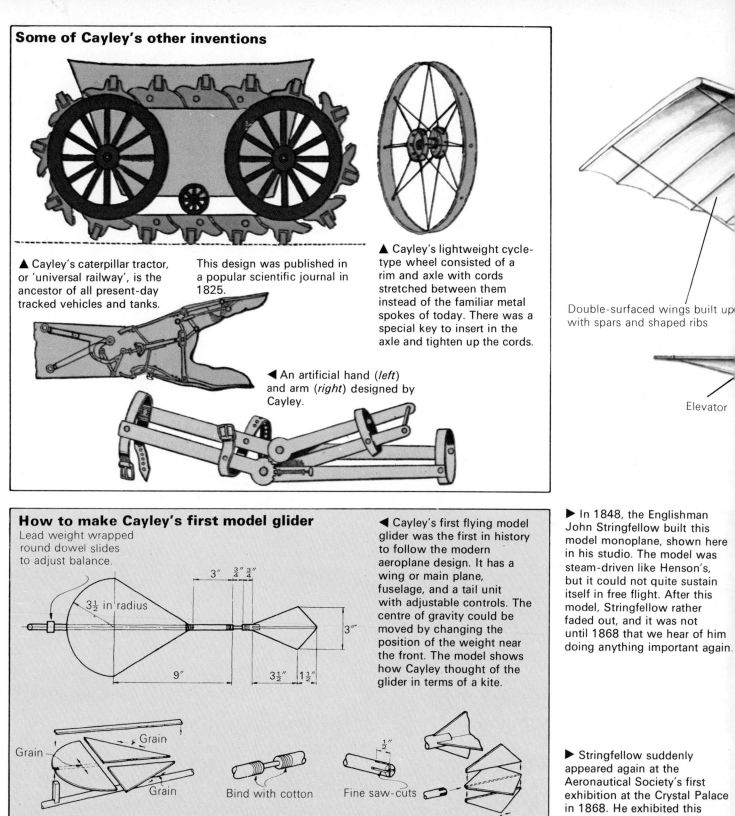

Some of Cayley's other inventions

▲ Cayley's caterpillar tractor, or 'universal railway', is the ancestor of all present-day tracked vehicles and tanks.

This design was published in a popular scientific journal in 1825.

▲ Cayley's lightweight cycle-type wheel consisted of a rim and axle with cords stretched between them instead of the familiar metal spokes of today. There was a special key to insert in the axle and tighten up the cords.

◀ An artificial hand (*left*) and arm (*right*) designed by Cayley.

Double-surfaced wings built up with spars and shaped ribs

Elevator

How to make Cayley's first model glider

Lead weight wrapped round dowel slides to adjust balance.

3½ in radius

3"   3" 3"
        ¾ ¾

9"   3½" 1½"

3"

Grain

Grain

Grain

Bind with cotton

Fine saw-cuts

½"

Grain

18 SWG wire. Bend to adjust trim.

Bind with cotton

1"

3"

15½"

1½" 4½"

1½"
1½"

0 1 2 3 4 5
Scale: inches

◀ Cayley's first flying model glider was the first in history to follow the modern aeroplane design. It has a wing or main plane, fuselage, and a tail unit with adjustable controls. The centre of gravity could be moved by changing the position of the weight near the front. The model shows how Cayley thought of the glider in terms of a kite.

Cayley's model can be copied at half scale in balsa wood by following the instructions on this diagram. The actual model used a common paper kite for the wing.

▶ In 1848, the Englishman John Stringfellow built this model monoplane, shown here in his studio. The model was steam-driven like Henson's, but it could not quite sustain itself in free flight. After this model, Stringfellow rather faded out, and it was not until 1868 that we hear of him doing anything important again.

▶ Stringfellow suddenly appeared again at the Aeronautical Society's first exhibition at the Crystal Palace in 1868. He exhibited this large model triplane, built at the suggestion — made long before — of the great Cayley himself. Cayley felt that a large spread of wing should be built in a number of 'decks' to provide a stronger structure than a single enormous wing. The model triplane could not sustain itself in the air, but it made many inventors begin to think along the right lines.

The Visionary Designers

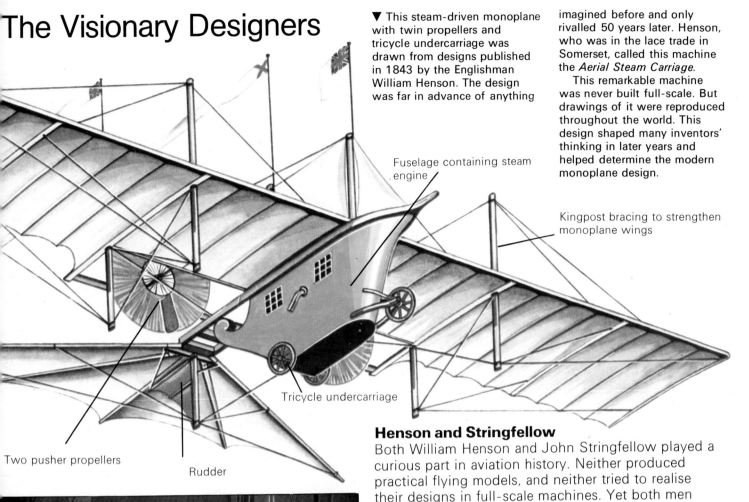

▼ This steam-driven monoplane with twin propellers and tricycle undercarriage was drawn from designs published in 1843 by the Englishman William Henson. The design was far in advance of anything imagined before and only rivalled 50 years later. Henson, who was in the lace trade in Somerset, called this machine the *Aerial Steam Carriage*.

This remarkable machine was never built full-scale. But drawings of it were reproduced throughout the world. This design shaped many inventors' thinking in later years and helped determine the modern monoplane design.

Fuselage containing steam engine

Kingpost bracing to strengthen monoplane wings

Tricycle undercarriage

Two pusher propellers

Rudder

Henson and Stringfellow

Both William Henson and John Stringfellow played a curious part in aviation history. Neither produced practical flying models, and neither tried to realise their designs in full-scale machines. Yet both men had a profound influence on aviation through the wide publicity given to their designs and models.

Pictures of Henson's 'Aerial Steam Carriage' appeared many hundreds of times in books and magazines all over the world. In 1847, Henson made a model from his design, and Stringfellow built a steam engine for the model. The model was tested but failed to sustain itself in flight. Henson then abandoned his model, married and emigrated to the U.S.A. in 1848.

In 1868, the Aeronautical Society of Great Britain — now the Royal Aeronautical Society — put on the world's first aeronautical exhibition at the Crystal Palace. There were 77 engines, models, drawings and other aeronautical items on show. Most of the exhibits concerning heavier-than-air flying were unpractical, but there is no doubt that the exhibition increased the enthusiasm for aviation.

Stringfellow exhibited a steam-driven model triplane at the Crystal Palace exhibition and attracted a great deal of technical interest. The design followed Cayley's suggestion that a large spread of wing should be built in several decks to provide a stronger structure. The performance of the model was a disappointment. It failed to fly, but influenced other designers to continue with triplanes and biplanes well into the 20th Century.

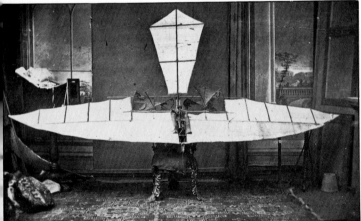

The Helicopter Craze

The helicopter is the oldest mechanical flying machine in the world. In model form, it certainly goes back to the 14th Century. In the 1860's and 70's there was a craze for building ingenious model helicopters. Unfortunately, there was no type of engine powerful yet light enough to raise both itself and a man into the air.

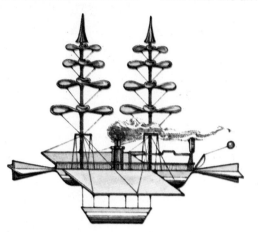

▲ Gabriel de La Landelle, a Frenchman who coined the word 'aviation', designed this dream-ship, which is typical of the amusing fantasies that appeared along with the serious models. It is a sort of steam-driven vertical-take-off aeroplane, with helicopter screws above rigid wings and a pusher airscrew at the back.

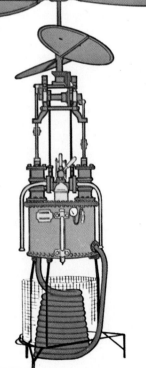

▶ An ingenious model helicopter was built in 1863 by Ponton d'Amecourt in France. It was steam-driven, with two contra-rotating rotors. But the excellent steam engine did not manage to lift the machine, and again it was made clear to the pioneers of the time that steam engines were far too heavy for the power they produced.

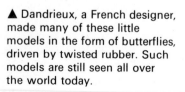

▲ Dandrieux, a French designer, made many of these little models in the form of butterflies, driven by twisted rubber. Such models are still seen all over the world today.

▲ This steam-driven model helicopter was built in 1877 by Enrico Forlanini, an Italian engineer. Its two rotors were contra-rotating (turning in opposite directions) and driven by steam generated in the sphere below. The sphere is a boiler, which was heated over a fire on the ground. When the temperature was high enough to produce enough steam, the model took off and flew upwards.

The Spread of 'Air-Mindedness'

People today accept air travel as an everyday event. They have become thoroughly 'air-minded'. But before the aeroplane became a practical vehicle in this century, aviation was in the hands of only a few experimenters and pioneers. The general public paid little attention and had to be gradually made aware of 'aerial voyaging', as it was then called. This was done by constant news of balloon flights and adventures, and later of the first attempts at flying lighter-than-air dirigibles.

Air-mindedness was also promoted by the thousands of flying toys available throughout the century. These included model helicopters and, eventually, model aeroplanes powered by twisted rubber, patterned after Alphonse Penaud's 'Planophore' of 1871.

One of the chief sources of inspiration towards aviation for the youth of Europe and America was the French author, Jules Verne. Verne's adventure books were translated and sold the world over. They included *Five weeks in a Balloon* and *Clipper of the Clouds*, in which the performance of his fantasy machine, the *Albatross*, foreshadowed that of present day helicopters.

Finally, in the latter part of the 19th Century, drawings and photographs were published of men like Lilienthal in Germany and Santos-Dumont in France in both lighter- and heavier-than-air flight. All of these factors helped to make the world air-minded and ready for the conquest of the air.

◀ Alphonse Penaud was a brilliant French aeronautical designer whose design for a full-sized amphibious monoplane was patented in 1876 but never built. The design included a glass-domed cockpit, a single control-column to operate the elevators and rudder, and a retractable undercarriage.

The French author Jules Verne (1828–1905) was a remarkable writer of aeronautical fiction who followed the progress of aviation closely.

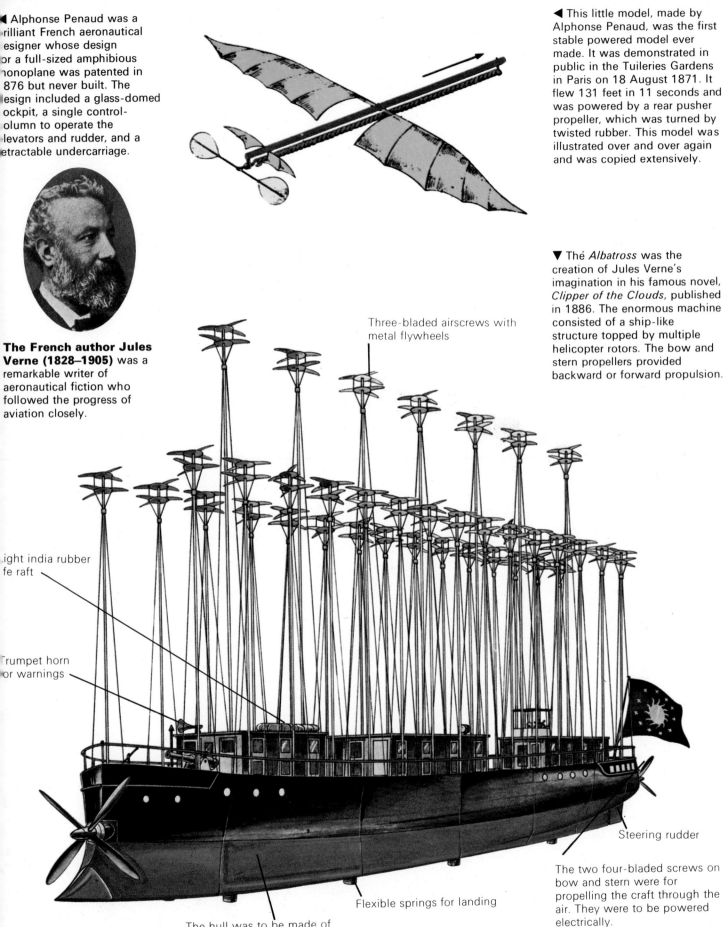

◀ This little model, made by Alphonse Penaud, was the first stable powered model ever made. It was demonstrated in public in the Tuileries Gardens in Paris on 18 August 1871. It flew 131 feet in 11 seconds and was powered by a rear pusher propeller, which was turned by twisted rubber. This model was illustrated over and over again and was copied extensively.

▼ The *Albatross* was the creation of Jules Verne's imagination in his famous novel, *Clipper of the Clouds*, published in 1886. The enormous machine consisted of a ship-like structure topped by multiple helicopter rotors. The bow and stern propellers provided backward or forward propulsion.

Three-bladed airscrews with metal flywheels

Light india rubber life raft

Trumpet horn for warnings

Steering rudder

The two four-bladed screws on bow and stern were for propelling the craft through the air. They were to be powered electrically.

Flexible springs for landing

The hull was to be made of 'compressed paper' for lightness.

First Take-Off

▶ The first manned machine to take off from level ground under its own power was the French engineer Clement Ader's steam-powered *Eole* in 1890. But it was only airborne for about 165 feet and could be neither sustained nor controlled in the air.

The huge four-bladed propeller appears to have been an imitation of birds' feathers although it was probably made from metal and wood. It was an inefficient shape. Ader had no real idea of the ideal shape for a propeller.

Du Temple had no proper method of stopping his aeroplane from rolling to one side or the other. Each wing was probably angled slightly upwards, but this would not have been adequate for complete stability.

Du Temple's engine was probably driven by steam. It would have been much too heavy to make an effective flying machine.

The rudder could be swung to the left and to the right.

▲ The first full-scale manned aeroplane to take off was designed by the Frenchman Felix Du Temple about 1874. It was steam-powered and took off after a down-ramp run. It could not sustain itself in the air.

This guard rail was to stop the machine rising more than a few inches off the railway track.

Maxim had a good light steam engine, but the complete machine weighed too much to fly properly.

This elevator was to enable the pilot to point the machine upwards or downwards.

▲ Sir Hiram Maxim built this steam-powered bi-plane test-rig. In 1894 the machine just raised itself from the rails, but could not fly in any proper sense of the word.

Ader built in all kinds of controls for his wings, including a device for swinging the wings back and forth in flight to alter the balance of the aeroplane. He would not have had time to operate these controls properly in the short time that he was airborne.

Ader had no tail on his aeroplane, which would have made directional control extremely difficult.

Ader's *Eole* had a very good light steam engine. Ader was an excellent steam engineer, but steam engines are too heavy for aeroplanes.

The tail elevator could be moved upwards and downwards.

▼ A Russian claim to the first flight has been put forward for the inventor Alexander Mozhaiski. He built this steam-powered monoplane and had it tested in 1884. But the machine could not fly. After careering down a 'ski-jump' ramp, it covered only a few yards under its own momentum before landing.

The upper wings were bent upwards at the ends to give some kind of stability in roll. The lower wings were bent upwards from the fuselage.

Chauffeurs and Gliders

During the last half of the 19th century, three main streams of inventors appeared. First, the model-makers, who did not attempt manned flight; then the 'chauffeurs' who tried to drive their powered machines into the air, with little or no idea of flight control; and lastly, the gliders, who tried to develop control of a glider in the air before venturing into powered flight.

Felix Du Temple belonged to both the model-making and the chauffeur schools of inventors. In 1857 or 1858, Du Temple built the first model aeroplane to take off under its own power and sustain itself in flight. About 1874, his full-size aeroplane made the world's first powered take-off after a run down an inclined ramp — not a true powered flight, but a creditable performance.

To make a successful powered flight, an aeroplane must be controllable, and must sustain itself in the air. For this reason, Clement Ader's take-off in the *Eole*, although the world's first from level ground, cannot be counted as the first true powered flight.

All the aeroplanes on this page made short trips, but they were all too heavy to fly properly, since they had to use steam engines. None of them were able to take advantage of the new four-stroke petrol engine perfected by the German engineer N.A. Otto in 1876, and later used so successfully by the Wrights. None of them had proper control systems, and none showed any real grasp of the importance of the curved wing shape, first demonstrated in 1884 by the British inventor H.F. Phillips.

These wires were to hold the wing up while the aeroplane was on the ground.

Man Learns to Fly

▲ Lilienthal made these patent drawings in 1893. On the right the glider's wings are shown folded for storage.

Otto Lilienthal (1848–96) was a German mechanical engineer who became the greatest pioneer of the pre-powered days. He built and flew both monoplane and biplane gliders and was the first man in history to rise in the air and truly fly.

These strong radiating spars could be hinged upwards for easy storage when the glider was not in use.

▶ Lilienthal is shown flying one of his monoplane gliders from his artificial hill in Berlin in 1894. The pilot was supported in the glider by his arms, which went through heavy leather cuffs. The flight of the glider was controlled by the pilot shifting the weight of his body and legs.

Lilienthal's artificial hill in Berlin had a hangar built into the top for storing gliders. From the top, Lilienthal could launch himself into the wind in any direction to obtain the longest gliding time. A flight path of a monoplane glider is shown.

Controlling a hang-glider The pilot takes off by leaping into the wind from the top of the hill, running and holding the machine almost horizontal.

The First Aviator

Otto Lilienthal was one of the greatest men in the history of flying and the first to undertake extensive experiments in the air. In 1889, he published a book on the methods of bird flight. He applied the results of his studies to human flight and especially to the problem of how much lift could be obtained from different wing areas.

His first gliding experiments were made from a springboard in 1891. The following years, he progressed to a gravel pit and then to some natural hills near Rhinow. In 1894, he had an artificial hill thrown up at Lichterfelde, a suburb of Berlin. The hill was about 50 feet high and allowed him to glide off into the wind in any direction.

All Lilienthal's machines were hang gliders with no movable control surfaces. The pilot was suspended by his arms so that he could move his body and legs in any direction to control the glider's flight. Lilienthal was aware of the limited control that this method provided. He suffered a severe crash, probably caused by being gusted to a halt in mid-air. The tail was thrust up by air pressure, and the glider went into a nose dive. After this, he devised a tailplane which hinged freely upwards but not downwards, which he thought would cure this problem.

Lilienthal built many monoplane gliders and three biplane versions. With these machines, he could make glides ranging from 300 to over 750 feet. At the time of his death, he was experimenting with a curious machine with flapping wing-tips powered by a carbonic-acid motor.

Lilienthal's career was particularly successful in inspiring others like the Wrights to follow his example. Dry-plate photography had been perfected by then, and many photographs were taken of him in the air and published throughout the world. Extracts from his writings were translated and widely read.

The hinged tailplane was the only movable surface on Lilienthal's gliders. It was not controlled by the pilot, but hinged freely upwards to lower the risk of a nose dive if the glider was gusted to a halt in the air.

The glider begins to dive too steeply. The pilot swings his weight toward the rear to bring the tail down and raise the nose.

The nose of the glider is gusted up. The pilot swings his body and legs forward to bring the nose down and prevent a stall.

One wing drops and the glider begins to side-slip. The pilot throws his weight to the same side as the raised wing to bring that side down.

Before landing, the pilot throws his weight backwards to raise the nose at the last minute, and then drops his legs to land.

Take-off from the edge of a gravel pit.

Legs forward to keep the nose down.

Legs thrown forward to bring the nose down for landing.

The willow hoop acted as a shock absorber in a crash.

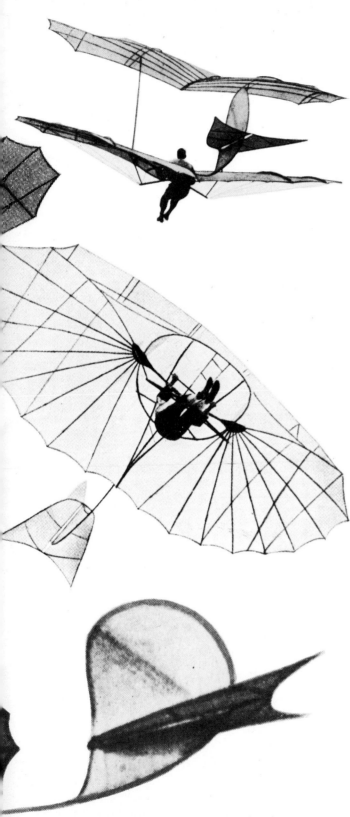

Take-off from the top of the artificial hill near Berlin.

Legs kicked back to raise the nose of the glider.

Landing at the foot of the artificial hill.

The photographs above show two of Lilienthal's biplane gliders. These and other photographs were published all over the world in the 1890's. They were taken with the sensitive dry-plate camera, which had only recently been perfected. These photographs brought the drama of flying to magazine readers and to the young men who would follow Lilienthal as pioneers of flight. The death of Lilienthal in a crash in 1896 helped influence the Wrights to take up flying.

A picnic after gliding. *(Lilienthal is second from right.)*

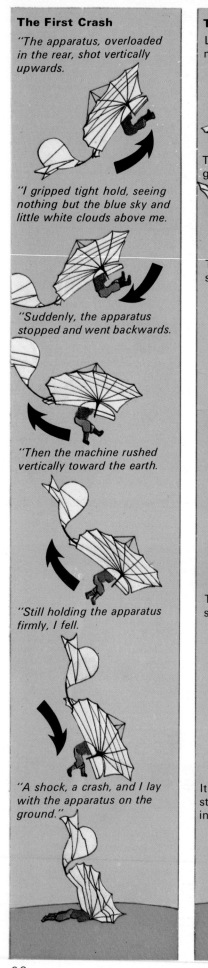

The First Crash

"The apparatus, overloaded in the rear, shot vertically upwards.

"I gripped tight hold, seeing nothing but the blue sky and little white clouds above me.

"Suddenly, the apparatus stopped and went backwards.

"Then the machine rushed vertically toward the earth.

"Still holding the apparatus firmly, I fell.

"A shock, a crash, and I lay with the apparatus on the ground."

The Fatal Crash

Lilienthal was gliding normally.

The nose of the glider was gusted up by the wind.

The machine stalled and the starboard wing dropped.

The glider lost lift and side-slipped.

It crashed, buckling the starboard wing and fatally injuring Lilienthal.

◀ Lilienthal had two serious crashes in his gliding career. In the first, described in his own words, he was saved by the willow hoop in front, which took the main force of the impact. In the second crash he was not so lucky, and his spine was broken in the fall.

▼ Percy Pilcher was killed while flying this glider, the *Hawk* in 1899.

The Death of Lilienthal

On 9 August 1896, a beautiful summer's day, Lilienthal was gliding from the hills at Gollenberg in one of his standard monoplanes. Suddenly, he was gusted to a standstill. The glider stalled and side-slipped to the ground, crumpling one wing but leaving the rest of the glider undamaged.

Lilienthal's spine was broken in the fall, and he died the next day.

Lilienthal was killed because he did not have sufficient control of his glider in flight. Shortly before he died, Lilienthal designed a controllable rear elevator, but it was not fitted to any of his gliders.

▼ This photograph of the actual plane in which Lilienthal was killed was taken in the courtyard of his factory.

The whole tail hinged freely
upwards from here, but it was
not controlled by the pilot.

Rigid fin and tailplane

▼ The Australian pioneer
Lawrence Hargrave invented
the stable box-kite in 1893.

▼ In Chanute's improved hang-
glider, the pilot could move his
weight backwards and forwards
on parallel bars.

▲ Hargrave also designed
powered models based on his
box-kite, such as this
multiplane in 1902.

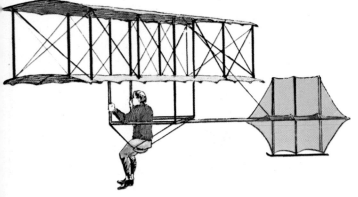

Hargrave, Chanute and Pilcher

The box-kite, invented by Lawrence Hargrave in 1893,
was important to aviation because it was very stable
in the air and had great lifting power. However, it was
not used in aeroplane design until 1905, when
Voisin made two box-kite float gliders.

Octave Chanute and Percy Pilcher were followers
of Otto Lilienthal. They made some advance on
Lilienthal in glider design, but neither built machines
with movable control surfaces, which could have
made the glider a practical vehicle.

Chanute, a French-American engineer, was too
old to fly himself, but the pilots of his hang gliders
never came to any harm. Pilcher was killed gliding in
1899 in a machine that had been left outside the night
before. One of the wooden tail members had been
soaked with rain and gave way in flight. The tail unit
buckled, the machine dived to earth, and Pilcher died
of his injuries.

If he had lived, Pilcher might have beaten the
Wrights in the race to build and fly the first powered
aeroplane. He had already designed a powered
machine. It would probably not have flown successfully,
but it could easily have led to a practical machine.

Control in the Air

Wing-warping moved this part of the wing up or down to raise or lower one side.

The single rear rudder was linked to the wing-warping controls so that both could be used together.

Wilbur Wright (1867–1912)

The Wright brothers became excellent engineers through self-training. In early life, they worked as printers, built their own presses and produced a local newspaper in Ohio. In 1892 they became interested in bicycles, and they began

Orville Wright (1871–1948)

selling and repairing them the following year. Eventually, they designed and manufactured their own cycles, the *Van Cleve* and the *Wright Special*. The cycle business supplied the money for their early flying experiments.

The elevator and pitch control

▲ The first Wright glider was tested as a kite in 1900. The elevator was for control of *pitch*, the up-and-down motion of the nose. The *angle of incidence* of the elevator — the angle of the elevator to the body of the glider — could be changed to make the glider climb or dive. The glider was also used to test the Wrights' method of wing-warping.

Wing warping and roll control

▲ Wing warping was a method of twisting the back edges of the wing ends upwards on one side and downwards on the other. The downward-twisted wing would then have more lift and would rise while the upward-twisted wing would sink. This *roll control* keeps the wings level or banks them for turning.

Pitch control

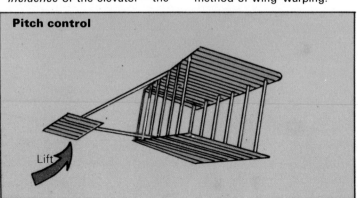

Lift

Roll control

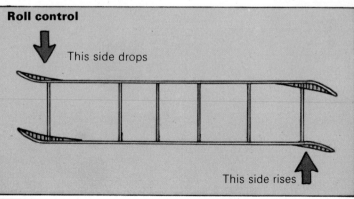

This side drops

This side rises

▼ The third Wright glider was flown at Kitty Hawk in 1902. The pilot lay in a gap in the lower wing. He worked the forward elevator control with his left hand and controlled the rudder and wing tips by swinging his hips from side to side in a movable cradle. He could turn by swinging his hips in the direction he wanted to turn.

The Wrights made over 1,000 glides in this machine during their 1902 season. Their distance record was 622½ feet, and their duration record 26 seconds.

The pilot lay with his hips in a cradle which operated the wing-warping and rudder controls.

The forward elevator was controlled by a hand lever.

The rudder and yaw control

▲ A rear rudder was used on the third Wright glider for control of yaw, or side-to-side motion. Turning the rudder to one side would turn the glider in the same direction. The rudder was used with wing warping to produce a banked turn to prevent a spin caused by the extra drag of the down-warped wing.

Yaw control

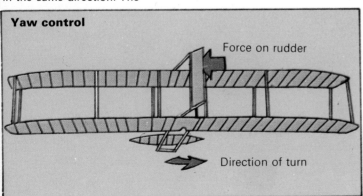

Force on rudder

Direction of turn

The Wrights Learn to Glide

After Lilienthal's death in 1896, the Wright brothers became more and more interested in flying. In 1899, they invented a method of roll control based on the way local buzzards twisted the tips of their wings to keep their balance in the air.

The Wrights' method was to give a greater angle of incidence to a wing that had dropped, and thus bring it level again, or to raise the wing above the level for a banked turn. They also felt that the righting and banking movements would be improved by twisting the other wing to a lower angle of incidence. They tested this idea in their kite of 1899, which had twistable wings. This wing-twisting became known as 'wing-warping'.

The Wrights decided that they must first master the art of gliding in an unpowered machine before trying to fly a machine with an engine. They chose to experiment at a remote area on the North Carolina coast, near Kitty Hawk. Here there were sand hills from which to glide and soft sand into which they could crash safely.

They perfected their gliding with their modified No. 3 glider in 1902. This machine combined roll control with rudder (yaw) control to produce smooth banked turns and to right itself if it was gusted over in flight. With their forward elevator, they then had full and proper flight control and were ready to build their first powered aeroplane.

The First Powered Flight

The Wright *Flyer I (right)* was the first aeroplane in the world to make powered, sustained and controlled flights and to land on ground as high as its take-off point. It was built in 1903 and made four flights on 17 December 1903 at the Kill Devil Hills, near Kitty Hawk, North Carolina.

The first flight lasted 12 seconds and covered 120 feet of ground or 500 feet in air distance, as the machine flew into a stiff breeze. The fourth and last flight of the day lasted 59 seconds and covered 852 feet of ground, or more than half a mile in air distance. The *Flyer I* took off from level ground and ran along a monorail under engine power alone until it became airborne.

12-hp Wright engine

The pilot lay prone and worked the controls in the same way as on the *No. 3* glider.

Both the forward biplane elevator and the rear rudder are very close to the wings. They were moved farther away in later *Flyers* for better flight control.

▲ The Wrights intended to use a standard motor car engine for their *Flyer*. But none of the manufacturers could supply engines light enough for a flying machine. So the brothers designed and built this engine. It had four cylinders lying horizontally, was water-cooled and gave about 12 horsepower. They installed it offset slightly to the starboard side to allow for the pilot lying amidships. The starboard wings were made slightly longer to compensate for the extra weight on that side.

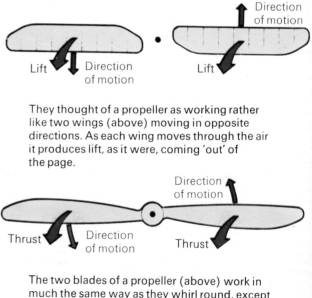

How the Wrights understood the propeller

The Wrights designed and built their own propellers, which were better than any previously designed.

Lift — Direction of motion

Direction of motion — Lift

They thought of a propeller as working rather like two wings (above) moving in opposite directions. As each wing moves through the air it produces lift, as it were, coming 'out' of the page.

Direction of motion

Thrust — Direction of motion — Thrust

The two blades of a propeller (above) work in much the same way as they whirl round, except that the force they produce is called thrust rather than lift.

The double rear rudder and the front biplane elevator were the principal differences between the *Flyer I* and the *No. 3* glider, which had a single rudder and elevator.

Warpable wings
Wing area: 510 sq ft
Wing span: 40 ft 4 in

The propellers were driven by a bicycle-chain drive, encased in tubes. One chain was crossed over so that one propeller would rotate in the opposite direction to the other. If both the propellers rotated in the same direction, the force of their movement (called torque) would unbalance the aeroplane.

Conquest of the Air

The Wrights' first powered machine, the *Flyer I*, was built during the summer of 1903. They transported it to the Kill Devil Hills in North Carolina and began their tests on 14 December 1903.

The Wrights tossed a coin to decide who should be the first pilot. Wilbur won, but the test was a failure. The *Flyer* climbed steeply, stalled and ploughed into the sand. It was December 17 before conditions were suitable for another test.

The Wrights made four flights on that momentous day. The longest covered 852 feet of ground, or over half a mile of air distance into the wind. Orville sent a telegram to his father, Bishop Wright, which read (including errors of transmission): SUCCESS FOUR FLIGHTS THURSDAY MORNING ALL AGAINST TWENTYONE MILE WIND STARTED FROM LEVEL WITH ENGINE POWER ALONE AVERAGE SPEED THROUGH AIR THIRTYONE MILES LONGEST 57 SECONDS INFORM PRESS HOME CHRISTMAS. OREVELLE WRIGHT. The 57 seconds should have read 59, and Orville's name was wrongly spelt.

This famous telegram was intercepted illegally while it was being relayed to Dayton, and a ridiculous and garbled story was given to the press. The press naturally treated it as a joke. Only a few references were made to the Wrights in the newspapers. The Wrights then wrote an account of their four flights and gave it to the Associated Press. But no one in America took them seriously.

The European pioneers had become bogged down in fruitless tests of unpractical machines. But they were well aware of the success of the three Wright gliders in 1900, 1901 and 1902. And they knew that the Wrights intended to put a petrol engine in a larger machine. So when the news arrived in Paris in 1903, it was obvious that the Americans had done what they said they would do.

▲ The most famous photograph in the history of aeronautics shows the *Flyer I* just after it became airborne for the first time. Orville is piloting while Wilbur runs alongside.

▲ In 1904, the Wrights built their second powered machine, the *Flyer II*. It was tested at the Huffman Prairie, near Dayton, Ohio, where the Wrights lived.

25

The First Practical Aeroplane

The Wright *Flyer III* of 1905 was the first practical powered aeroplane in history. It could bank, turn, circle, fly figures of eight, and remain in the air for over half an hour at a time. It was also robust enough to stand any number of take-offs and landings. It was flown at the Huffman Prairie, near Dayton, Ohio, for more than 40 flights in 1905.

The brothers offered their machine three times to the U.S. Government. Each time, the offer was turned down because the military authorities could not believe that such a machine could have been built by two brothers in a small town like Dayton. They told themselves that the Wrights only wanted money for experiments, not for a working aeroplane. Then they told the Wrights that they could not provide money for experiments.

This refusal so angered the brothers that they offered their invention to the British Government. But this offer also fell through because the Wrights refused to show their plane to any buyer before an agreement was arranged to purchase it. They stated plainly that the Government need not purchase the *Flyer* unless it performed as they said it would. Even then, the British Government would not consider the purchase until they had seen the plane.

By late 1905, the brothers were so concerned with secrecy that they refused to fly in public until they could make a business agreement. This took time, and they did no flying until 1908, when they made agreements with the U.S. Army and a commercial firm in France.

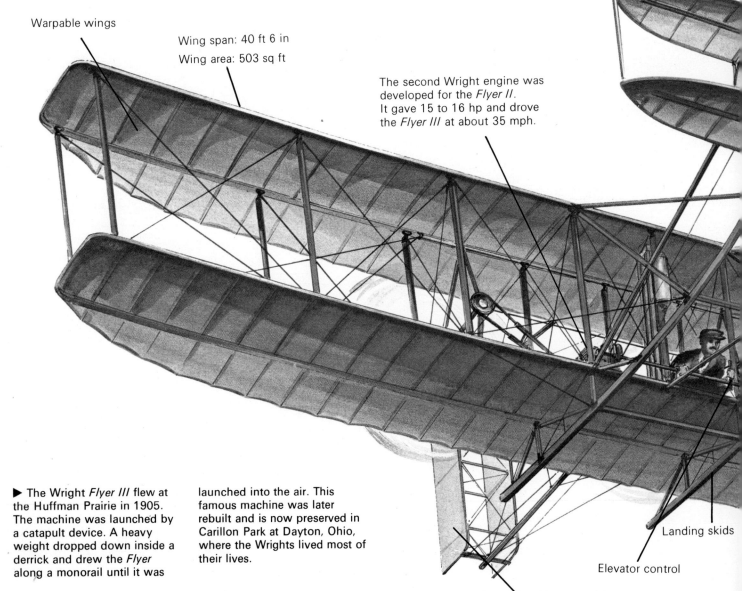

Warpable wings

Wing span: 40 ft 6 in
Wing area: 503 sq ft

The second Wright engine was developed for the *Flyer II*.
It gave 15 to 16 hp and drove the *Flyer III* at about 35 mph.

Landing skids

Elevator control

Double rear rudder

▶ The Wright *Flyer III* flew at the Huffman Prairie in 1905. The machine was launched by a catapult device. A heavy weight dropped down inside a derrick and drew the *Flyer* along a monorail until it was launched into the air. This famous machine was later rebuilt and is now preserved in Carillon Park at Dayton, Ohio, where the Wrights lived most of their lives.

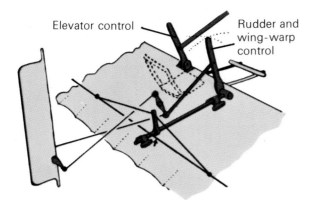

Elevator control

Rudder and wing-warp control

▲ This is the control system finally developed for the Wright *Flyers*. A single lever worked the forward elevator, and another lever worked both the warping wires and the rudder.

The second lever replaced the hip cradle. It could be moved in any direction to combine wing-warping and movement of the rear rudder.

Both the elevator and the rudder were made larger and moved farther from the wings than on earlier models

These half-moon 'blinkers' were added to provide keel area and aid yaw control.

This tow-rod was used for the derrick-assisted launch from a monorail.

Langley's Aerodrome

Samuel Pierpont Langley, a famous American scientist, was the Wrights' only serious rival. In 1903, he built a tandem-wing monoplane. He wrongly named it the *Aerodrome*, a word only to be used for an airfield. He launched it twice from a houseboat on the Potomac River, near Washington, D.C.

The *Aerodrome* had some good qualities, but its structure was not sound, the aerodynamics had not been worked out properly and the control system was unreliable.

Langley's pilot, Charles Manly, was lucky to escape with his life on both launches. He sat too low in the plane, and, if it had flown, he would have been in danger when it landed.

▲ The *Aerodrome* was launched by catapult from the houseboat in October and December 1903.

It crashed both times, but the pilot was rescued unhurt from the river.

▲ The first launch and crash of the *Aerodrome*.

▼ The second crash.

Europe Learns to Fly

After the death of Lilienthal in 1896, European aviation almost went to sleep. Then, news of the Wright brothers' gliding in the years 1900–02 gave a new impetus to work in Europe. But the Europeans proved to be very slow and slapdash in their flying experiments. It was not until the end of 1907 that any European aeroplane could stay in the air for even a single minute, whereas the Wrights had been flying for over half an hour at a time in 1905.

The chief trouble with the European pioneers was that they would never stick to one idea and see it through to success. They never fully understood the importance of learning to fly and control a glider before building powered machines. It was lucky that they were so slow in succeeding to fly, because if any of the early European aviators had got into the air in a powered aeroplane, they would not have known what to do with it once it was airborne!

In 1905, a newcomer to aviation, Gabriel Voisin, started to build aeroplanes with his brother Charles. They built sometimes to the designs of others and sometimes with a mixture of their own and their clients' ideas. The Voisins built two box-kite float-gliders in 1905. By the end of 1907 they were building powered machines, which were not successful until the following year. Meanwhile, Alberto Santos-Dumont, a Brazilian, made the first hop-flights in Europe in 1906 near Paris.

At the end of 1907, Henry Farman, an expatriate Englishman who lived in France, bought a Voisin aeroplane and began to modify it. By January of 1908, he had made it one of the first moderately successful machines in Europe. Farman was later to become the most famous of the biplane pilots, rivalled only by Bleriot and Latham in their monoplanes.

▼ Horatio Phillips made a few short hop-flights on this multi-slat aeroplane in 1907. The machine could not fly properly and Phillips abandoned it.

▶ This is the Voisin machine which Henry Farman bought in 1907 and modified. On it, he made the first circle in the air in Europe on 13 January 1908. Although Farman had carried out some valuable modifications, this aircraft was still a primitive machine. It had no control in roll by ailerons or wing-warping, which made it very difficult to turn safely.

This box-kite tail unit was later modified to a smaller version by Farman.

The rudder is concealed between the fixed side curtains.

▲ Ernest Archdeacon was a rich Parisian lawyer who did not fly himself, but who encouraged and paid for others to experiment. After having two unsuccessful gliders built for him, he commissioned Gabriel Voisin to build this float-glider. It was based on Hargrave's box-kite and was a failure, but it led the way to better planes later.

▼ Paul Cornu made the first brief free vertical take-off with this odd-looking helicopter in 1907 in France.

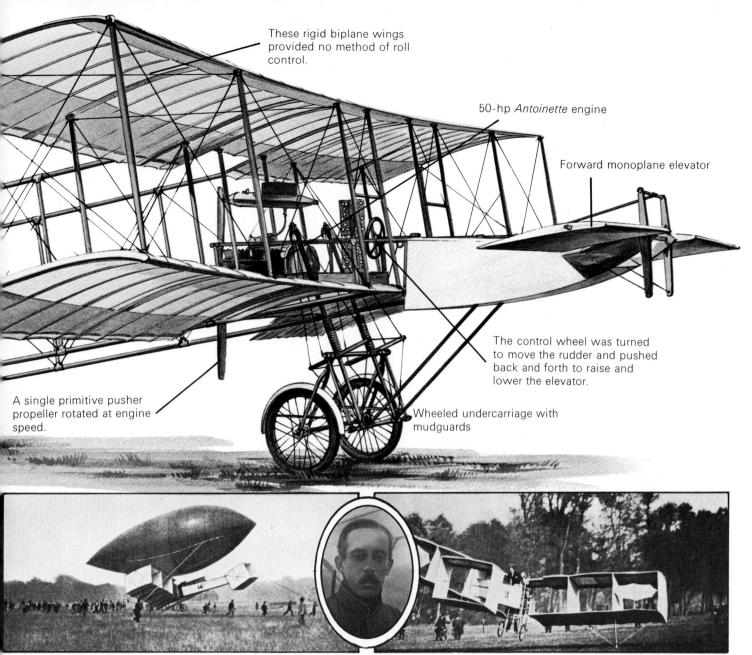

These rigid biplane wings provided no method of roll control.

50-hp *Antoinette* engine

Forward monoplane elevator

The control wheel was turned to move the rudder and pushed back and forth to raise and lower the elevator.

A single primitive pusher propeller rotated at engine speed.

Wheeled undercarriage with mudguards

▲ Alberto Santos-Dumont was a rich Brazilian who lived in Paris. He was interested in balloons and airships before he took up heavier-than-air powered machines. This clumsy machine, the '14-*bis*', was first tested by hanging it from one of his airships.

▲ The 14-*bis* succeeded in making the first official flights in Europe under its own power at the end of 1906. But the flights were really only long hops. Using a 50-horsepower Antoinette engine, the 14-bis managed to stay in the air for a brief 21 seconds. The machine flew 'tail first', with its combined elevator and rudder out in front of the wings.

► The first European aircraft manufacturers were the two Voisin brothers, Gabriel (*left*) and Charles. From 1907 onwards, they built a large number of biplanes which were safe but very primitive. The Voisin planes could only be flown in very calm weather, as they had no roll-control by ailerons or wing-warping. Many Europeans had their first lessons in flying these machines. They were easy to fly and safe, if the pilot kept low down and did not try any manoeuvres.

The First Monoplanes

The monoplane, or single-wing aeroplane, was the design most widely known throughout the early history of aviation. It began with Cayley's design for a powered monoplane in 1799. Henson's *Aerial Steam Carriage* of 1843 gave the monoplane its familiar appearance of main planes, fuselage, undercarriage, propellers and tail-unit.

Practical powered flying was first achieved by the biplane. which was a convenient way of obtaining a large wing area in a comparatively small and rigid structure. But the champions of the monoplane emerged as early as 1906. The beginning of the European monoplane tradition was an unsuccessful machine by Trajan Vuia in 1906. This was followed by the prophetic — though also unsuccessful — monoplane built by Bleriot in 1907, which he called his *No. VII*.

In 1908, the first of Leon Levavasseur's graceful monoplanes appeared, the *Gastambide-Mengin I*. This was later to lead to the *Antoinettes*, the chief rivals to the Bleriot machines. No monoplane flew properly until 1909, when these two models competed for popularity.

The monoplane and the biplane were equally successful for a year or two. But, in 1912, an unfounded suspicion arose that monoplanes were unsafe, and this type went into temporary decline.

After Wilbur Wright's demonstration in Europe in 1908, both monoplane and biplane designers took to Wright-type wing-warping or ailerons for control in roll. Both systems were in use until the start of World War I, when ailerons finally won the day.

◄ The *Gastambide-Mengin I*, built in 1908, was not successful in itself, but led to the great series of *Antoinette* monoplanes. It was designed by the Frenchman Leon Levavasseur (*right*), who also designed the *Antoinette* engines. Both aircraft and engines were named after Antoinette Gastambide, the daughter of the head of the company.

◄ The *Bleriot VII* of 1907 was not itself successful but led to great things later on. This is the form of monoplane that was to become familiar the world over, with tractor (i.e., front) propeller, main planes, covered-in fuselage, and tail-unit of rudder and elevators.

▲ Levavasseur's *Antoinette* engines were the most popular aeroplane engines in Europe. They had eight cylinders and came with 24 or 50 horsepower

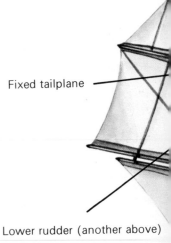

Fixed tailplane

Lower rudder (another above)

▼ The *Antoinette IV* of 1908 was one of the most graceful aeroplanes in history. It was used in the first try to cross the English Channel. The engine failed, and the pilot, Hubert Latham, had to land on the water. He was unhurt, and the machine was salvaged.

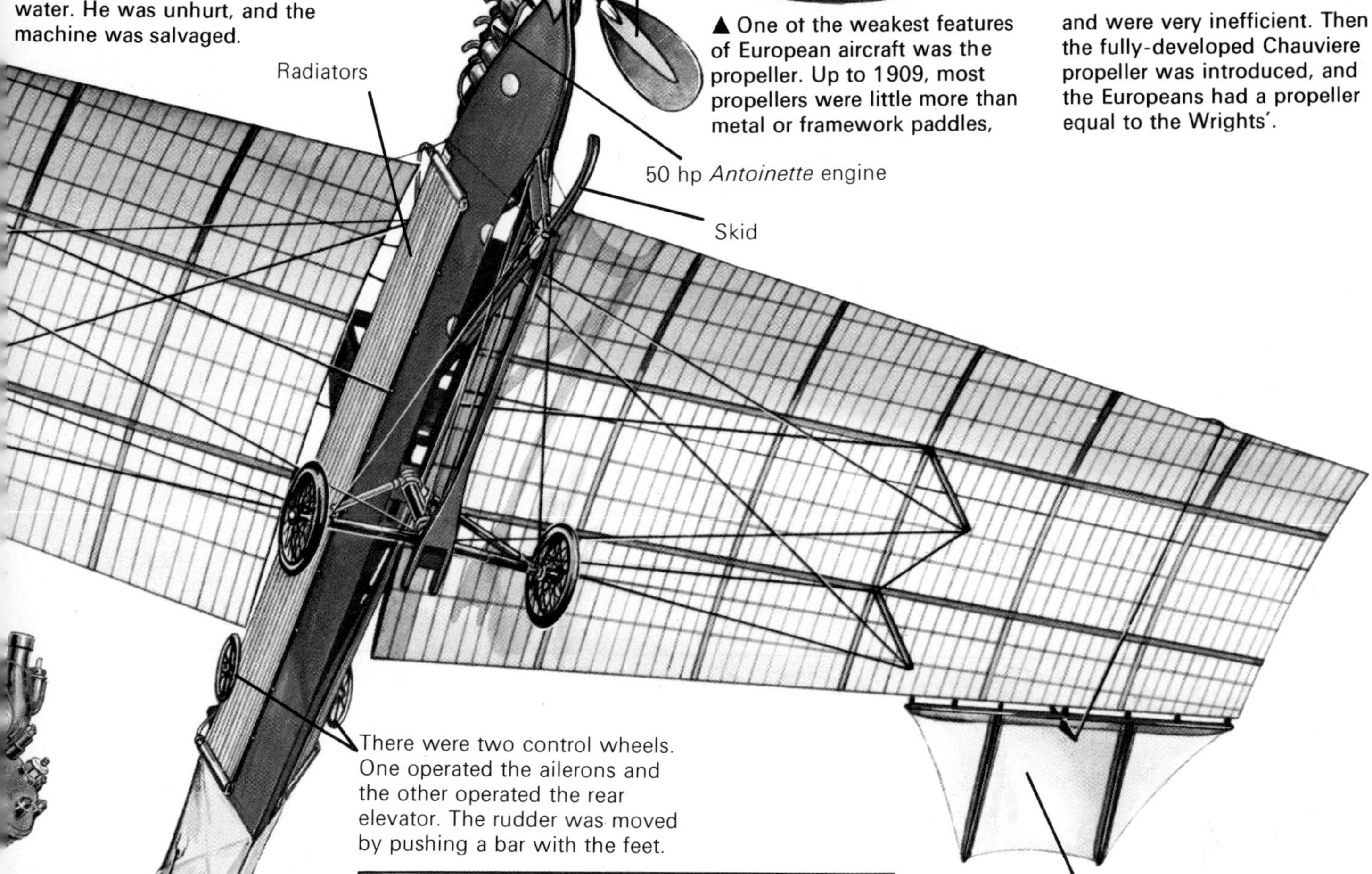

Primitive paddle-blade propeller

▲ One ot the weakest features of European aircraft was the propeller. Up to 1909, most propellers were little more than metal or framework paddles, and were very inefficient. Then the fully-developed Chauviere propeller was introduced, and the Europeans had a propeller equal to the Wrights'.

Radiators

50 hp *Antoinette* engine

Skid

There were two control wheels. One operated the ailerons and the other operated the rear elevator. The rudder was moved by pushing a bar with the feet.

This model had ailerons for roll control. Other *Antoinettes* used wing-warping.

◀ The French engineer Robert Esnault-Pelterie designed his first monoplane in 1907 and also built the engine. It was not successful, but it led to better machines of the same type.

▼ Also in 1907, Santos-Dumont built the forerunner of all light planes, his *No. 19*, with a bamboo frame. It was not successful until 1909, when it was called the *Demoiselle*.

Rear elevator

Wilbur in Europe

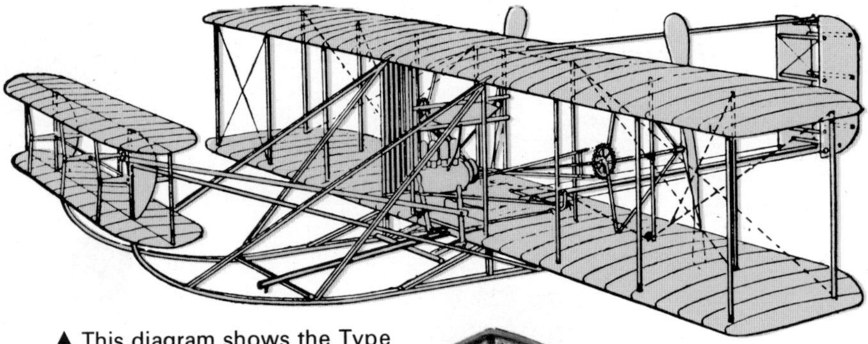

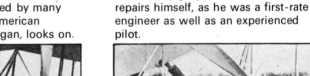

▼ This drawing is taken from a photograph of the *Wright A* coming in to land at the small race-course at Hunaudieres, near Le Mans in France. Wilbur made his first flight there in August 1908. He was soon allowed to transfer his flying to the great military ground of Auvours, also near Le Mans.

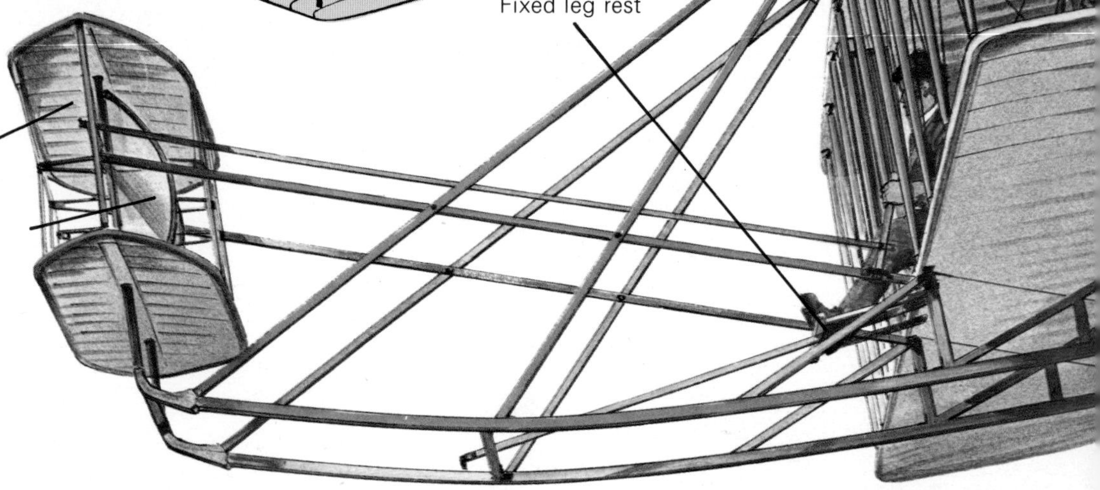

Fixed leg rest

▲ This diagram shows the Type A machine which Wilbur Wright brought to Europe and flew triumphantly in 1908.

Forward biplane elevator

Two blinkers to provide keel area

▼ Wilbur Wright flying his machine in a circuit of the Hunaudieres race-course.

▼ In 1909, Wilbur moved to the French resort of Pau and was visited by many famous people. Here, an American heiress, Miss Pierpont Morgan, looks on.

▼ Wilbur (*right*) carried out all the repairs himself, as he was a first-rate engineer as well as an experienced pilot.

▼ It was always considered a privilege to help pull up the weight inside the derrick used to launch the Wright machines. The heavy weight was triggered by the pilot and dropped down inside the derrick.

▼ The weight was attached to a rope which pulled the aeroplane forward until it rose into the air.

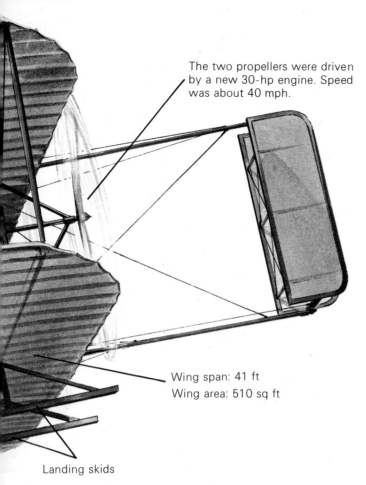

The two propellers were driven by a new 30-hp engine. Speed was about 40 mph.

Wing span: 41 ft
Wing area: 510 sq ft

Landing skids

The Wright A in France

After long delays and bargaining, a French company met the Wright brothers' terms for the building of one of their aeroplanes. Wilbur Wright went to France to fly his machine in public for the first time.

The first European flights of the Wright biplane caused a great sensation. Wilbur's mastery of flight control had a strong impact on the still struggling European pioneers. For the first time, the French airmen realised the importance of proper roll control. They were astounded to see Wilbur, in perfect command of his aeroplane, banking and flying in circles and figures of eight.

The Wrights' method of flight control taught the Europeans the last important lesson they had yet to learn. They were also astonished at the Wrights' comparatively low-powered engine, which drove two propellers geared down to less than engine speed. The European 50 horsepower engines drove their primitive propellers directly at engine speed.

There was much criticism of the Wrights' launching method, which depended upon a monorail catapult take-off. But the Wright machine could take off without the catapult if necessary. Since there were as yet only a few prepared grounds, it was better to land on skids than to risk overturning with a wheeled undercarriage on rough ground. Later, four small wheels were fitted to the skids and the machine took off easily from smooth ground.

Wilbur broke every flying record set before. From August to the end of December 1908, he was airborne for about 26 hours, and made many passenger flights and long-distance solo flights, ending with a wonderful duration-flight of 2 hours and 20 minutes.

The French, after being suspicious of the Wrights' claims, admitted the superiority of the *Wright A*. Bleriot was moved to say: "For us in France, and everywhere, a new era of mechanical flight has commenced." Major B. F. S. Baden-Powell, brother of the Chief Scout, said: "That Wilbur Wright is in possession of a power which controls the fate of nations is beyond dispute."

▼ When Wilbur took up women passengers, their blowing skirts could be a dangerous hazard to flying. So Wilbur tied a piece of string round the skirt before he took Madame Hart O. Berg up for a flight.

▼ When Wilbur raised the nose, the pin of the tow-rod was pulled off the tow-rope, and the machine flew free.

▼ A famous caricature of well-known people in France helping to pull up the weight. Wilbur stands at the far right in his usual cap.

Flying the Wright A

Learning to fly a Wright biplane was not difficult. The enemies of the Wrights liked to say that their machines could only be flown by acrobats. This was nonsense, but most pilots needed a week or two of instruction to gain the coordination necessary to fly the machine.

The flying controls were:
1. The forward elevator stick by the instructor's left knee;
2. The wing-warp and rudder stick between the two aviators;
3. A duplicate elevator stick for the pupil by his right knee. On these pages, the flying instructions are given for the sticks at the instructor's seat.

▲ Wilbur Wright is shown at the controls of his *Wright A*.

The pupil sat at Wilbur's right in the second seat (*arrow*).

Using the left-hand stick

▼ For level flight, the pilot holds the forward elevator parallel to the ground.

▼ To climb, the pilot pulls back the left-hand stick to raise the elevator.

▼ To dive, the pilot pushes the left-hand stick forwards to tilt the elevator down.

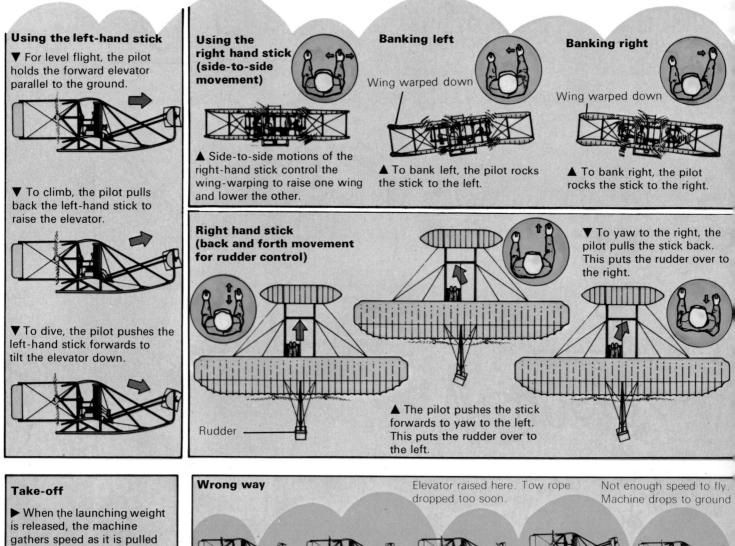

Using the right hand stick (side-to-side movement)

▲ Side-to-side motions of the right-hand stick control the wing-warping to raise one wing and lower the other.

Banking left

Wing warped down

▲ To bank left, the pilot rocks the stick to the left.

Banking right

Wing warped down

▲ To bank right, the pilot rocks the stick to the right.

Right hand stick (back and forth movement for rudder control)

Rudder

▲ The pilot pushes the stick forwards to yaw to the left. This puts the rudder over to the left.

▼ To yaw to the right, the pilot pulls the stick back. This puts the rudder over to the right.

Take-off

▶ When the launching weight is released, the machine gathers speed as it is pulled down the monorail. If the pilot raises the elevator too soon (*top strip*), the machine will rise and slip free of the tow rope before it is moving fast enough to fly. The pilot should hold the elevator slightly down until he reaches the end of the rail (*lower strip*). He then raises the elevator to climb into the air.

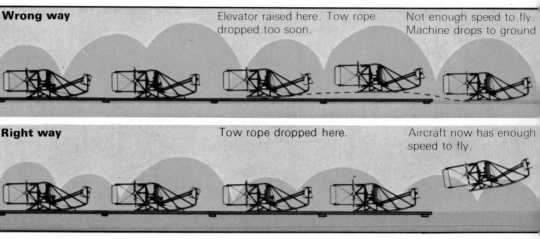

Wrong way   Elevator raised here. Tow rope dropped too soon.   Not enough speed to fly. Machine drops to ground

Right way   Tow rope dropped here.   Aircraft now has enough speed to fly.

Levelling out (wrong way)

▶ A dangerous situation can arise if the machine is gusted over and begins to roll. If the pilot tries to level it simply by down-warping the dropped wing, then the extra drag on that wing may swing the machine around and out of control. In the extreme case, the biplane will side-slip and crash.

(Machine is flying towards you.)

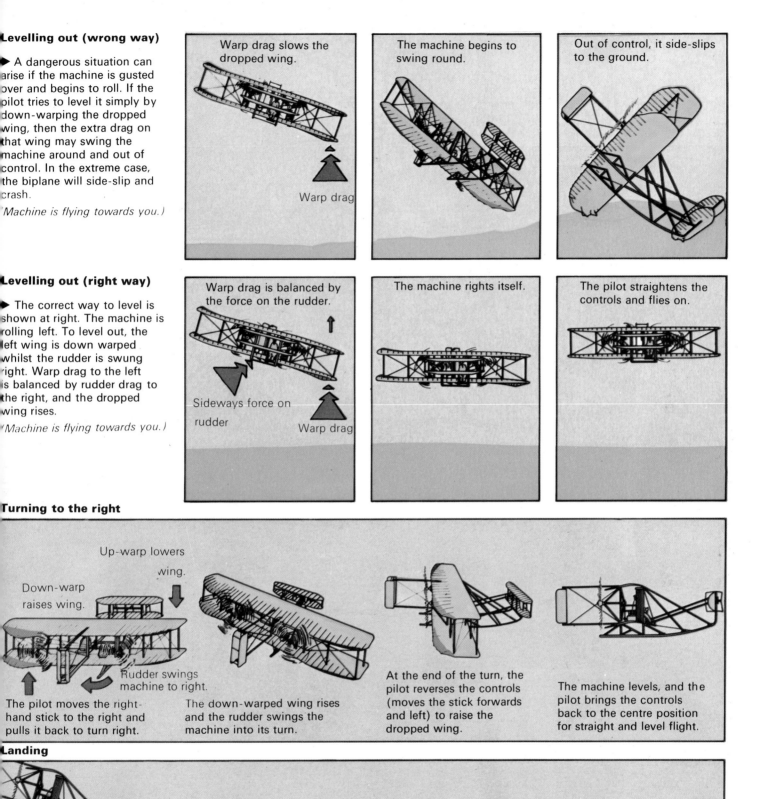

Warp drag slows the dropped wing.

Warp drag

The machine begins to swing round.

Out of control, it side-slips to the ground.

Levelling out (right way)

▶ The correct way to level is shown at right. The machine is rolling left. To level out, the left wing is down warped whilst the rudder is swung right. Warp drag to the left is balanced by rudder drag to the right, and the dropped wing rises.

(Machine is flying towards you.)

Warp drag is balanced by the force on the rudder.

Sideways force on rudder

Warp drag

The machine rights itself.

The pilot straightens the controls and flies on.

Turning to the right

Down-warp raises wing.

Up-warp lowers wing.

Rudder swings machine to right.

The pilot moves the right-hand stick to the right and pulls it back to turn right.

The down-warped wing rises and the rudder swings the machine into its turn.

At the end of the turn, the pilot reverses the controls (moves the stick forwards and left) to raise the dropped wing.

The machine levels, and the pilot brings the controls back to the centre position for straight and level flight.

Landing

For landing, the pilot pushes the left-hand stick forwards to depress the elevator.

As he nears the ground, the pilot slowly straightens the elevator.

At the last minute, he raises the elevator to put the nose up and cuts the engine at the same time.

The machine then sinks easily and gently to the ground.

35

Orville in America

▲ Orville took Major G. O. Squier for a flight on 12 September 1908 at Fort Myer.

Orville's fine flying convinced everyone in America that the Wrights had conquered the air.

◄ The ill-fated Lieutenant Selfridge (*left*) is shown here with Dr. Graham Bell, inventor of the telephone and backer of the Aerial Experiment Association. Despite Selfridge's death, the U.S. Army was convinced that the machine was outstanding and invited Orville to fly again.

▲ The Wrights did not fly between the end of 1905 and the beginning of 1908, while they were vainly trying to get commercial agreements to build their aircraft. They succeeded in doing this by 1908, and Wilbur flew in the most spectacular way in France.

Meanwhile, an agreement had also been reached with the United States Army. Orville remained in America to carry out the official tests at Fort Myer, near Washington, D.C.

These flights would surely · have been as brilliant as Wilbur's, if tragedy had not

struck on 17 September 1908. Orville had started flying on 3 September. During the next few days he made ten flights and was airborne for just under six hours. He made four flights of just over an hour each, and three passenger flights.

On the 17th, Orville was

flying with Lieutenant T. E. Selfridge as passenger when a split developed in a blade of the starboard propeller. This blade flattened and lost thrust, and the whole propeller got out of balance and tore loose its outrigger. Then the waving propeller hit and sliced through

▶ The *June Bug* was flown by its designer, Glenn Curtiss, on the first public flight in America on 4 July 1908. The flight covered just over 5000 feet, and the machine was not successful.

▲ **Glenn Curtiss (1878–1930)** was the most successful designer and pilot of the American 'Aerial Experiment Association' (A.E.A.). His chief talent was in adapting other men's inventions and making them work successfully, though he showed great originality in engine building. He soon broke away from the A.E.A. and made a name for himself as the greatest early American pilot after the Wrights. By the time of the Reims airshow in 1909, he had a very fine aeroplane in his *Golden Flier*. He later developed the first practical seaplane in history. He hated the Wrights and tried unsuccessfully to show that Langley's *Aerodrome* of 1903 could have flown before the Wright *Flyer*.

The Wrights and Their Competitors

In the United States, competition for the Wrights came from a new group called the 'Aerial Experiment Association', which was founded by Mrs and Dr Graham Bell, Glenn Curtiss, Lieutenant Selfridge and others. To avoid infringing the Wrights' patent, they followed Robert Esnault-Pelterie in adopting ailerons instead of wing-warping for roll control. They did not make a thorough study of aerodynamics as the Wrights had done. Instead, they gave up glider experiments almost at once and plunged ahead with designing and trying to fly powered machines.

It was not until Glenn Curtiss designed and flew the A.E.A.'s *June Bug* that there was much success. The chief achievement of the A.E.A. was to launch Curtiss on his aeronautical career as designer, constructor, pilot and engine builder.

After the accident in which Selfridge was killed at Fort Myer, Orville made a good recovery and was ready for further Army trials the next year (1909). A special machine was built, now called the *Wright A (Signal Corps)*, and Orville returned to Fort Myer and won the Army contract in July. Meanwhile, Wilbur finished training three French pilots at Pau in France and then went on to give a fine demonstration with his machine just outside Rome.

a bracing wire to the tail, which collapsed, sending the machine into a dive. Orville almost managed to bring up the nose, but the machine crashed to the ground, killing Selfridge and injuring Orville.

▶ The *Red Wing* was the first A.E.A. machine. It made only two hop-flights before it crashed and was abandoned. It was designed by Lt. Selfridge.

Across the English Channel

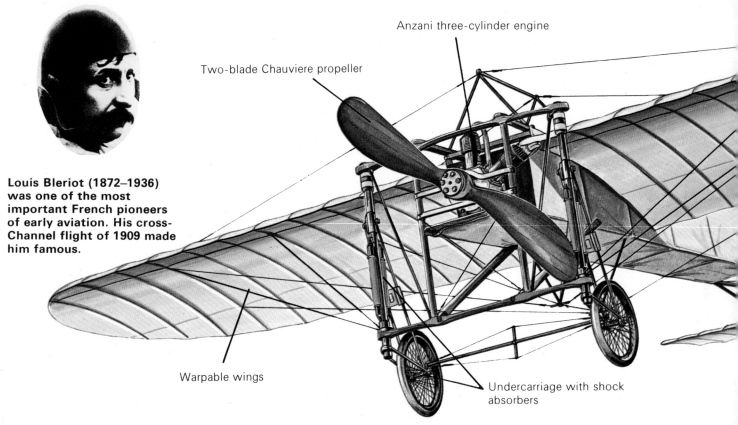

Louis Bleriot (1872–1936) was one of the most important French pioneers of early aviation. His cross-Channel flight of 1909 made him famous.

Two-blade Chauviere propeller

Anzani three-cylinder engine

Warpable wings

Undercarriage with shock absorbers

"HOW I FLEW THE CHANNEL"

"At 4.35 I gave my mechanics the order to let go. I struck out across the dunes and went over the telegraph wires at a height of about 180 ft. I could see the destroyer *Escopette* a few miles out at sea, and I took my bearing from her.

"The destroyer was steaming at full speed, but I very quickly passed her. My machine was then travelling at about 45 miles an hour. I wished to keep the monoplane at 250 ft, as that would be suitable for landing at the point on the cliff which had been selected.

"Then I lost sight of the *Escopette* and everything – the English land was not in view. The flight continued for about ten minutes with nothing in sight but sea and sky. It was the most anxious part of the flight, as I had no certainty that my direction was correct.

"At last I sighted the outline of the land, but I was then going in the direction of Deal. In setting my steering I had overlooked the effect of the wind, which was blowing rather strongly from the south-west. I therefore headed my monoplane westward. I could see a fleet of battleships in Dover Harbour, and I flew over these to a point where I could see my friend Monsieur Fontaine, with a large French tricolour, denoting the point where I was to descend.

"I flew over the cliffs all right, but the descent was one of the most difficult I have ever made. I circled round twice to ease the descent, but alighted more heavily than I expected to, and the monoplane was damaged."

From a contemporary newspaper account.

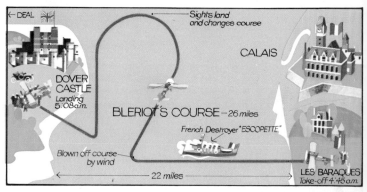

DEAL

Sights land and changes course

CALAIS

DOVER CASTLE
Landing 5.08 a.m.

BLERIOT'S COURSE – 26 miles

French Destroyer "ESCOPETTE"

Blown off course by wind

22 miles

LES BARAQUES
Take-off 4.45 a.m.

▲ Bleriot was blown off course by the wind and had to loop back to land at Dover Castle. He was accompanied by the French destroyer *Escopette* in case of an engine failure.

▼ After landing, Bleriot talked with the *Daily Mail* reporter and Monsieur Fontaine, whose large French flag is stuck firmly in front of the tailplane to prevent the machine running downhill.

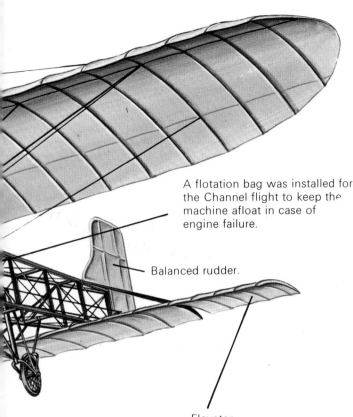

A flotation bag was installed for the Channel flight to keep the machine afloat in case of engine failure.

Balanced rudder.

Elevator

◄ The small and rather frail monoplane which took Bleriot across the English Channel on 25 July 1909 was his *No. XI*. This historic machine started as a rather primitive affair with an REP engine and an inefficient propeller. By the time it flew the Channel, it had an excellent Chauviere propeller and a small but reliable three-cylinder Anzani engine.

The crossing was a very lucky occasion, for even the best European engines had a habit of breaking down at the wrong moment, as Latham's *Antoinette* engine did in his earlier bid to cross the Channel. The *No. XI* was not really a robust enough machine in which to try such a hazardous flight.

▲ The man who tried first to fly the Channel was the Anglo-French Hubert Latham, who set out from Sangatte in France on 19 July in his *Antoinette IV*. His engine failed seven miles out to sea. He was accompanied by the French destroyer *Harpon*, which rescued him and the damaged *Antoinette*.

Louis Bleriot

Louis Bleriot made a large amount of money by inventing and making the famous Bleriot acetylene motor car headlamps, which were sold all over Europe. He had been interested in flying for some years, when, in 1905, he commissioned Gabriel Voisin to build him a float glider, which was not successful. In 1907, he had three different aeroplanes built, and by the end of 1908 his machines were making some creditable flights.

Bleriot eventually adopted the monoplane design for all his machines and had considerable success before he entered for the London *Daily Mail's* £1000 prize for the first cross-Channel flight. He did this only after Hubert Latham had failed in his attempt on an *Antoinette* on 19 July.

Bleriot showed great bravery and toughness in attempting the cross-Channel flight in his frail *No. XI* monoplane with its small 25-horsepower Anzani engine. "No pilot of today, no matter how great, could repeat this exploit in such an aircraft and with such an engine," says the historian Charles Dollfus. But luck was with Bleriot, and he triumphed. Overnight, he became one of the world's popular heroes.

Bleriot's success made all the European governments very much afraid that the aeroplane might one day be used for military invasions. His success also brought over 100 orders for his *No. XI* aircraft, so the large amount of money he had spent on flying came back to him with the triumph of his Channel crossing.

▲ A tumultuous reception was given to Bleriot when he arrived at Victoria Station, London, on the way to a lunch in his honour at the Savoy Hotel on 26 July 1909.

▼ Bleriot and his wife stand in front of the famous *No. XI* machine. The wings are removed and attached to the fuselage for transport..

The Champagne Airshow

The first great aviation meeting of history was held from 22 to 29 August 1909 on the plain of Bethany, north of Reims in the Champagne district of France. The meeting was a great success and proved that the aeroplane had indeed arrived.

▲ The *Wright A* performed magnificent banked turns round the pylons of the flying course at Reims. Eugene Lefebvre was the pilot.

▼ This famous aviation poster was issued to advertise the world's first great air meeting. The aeroplanes and balloons are shown flying over the cathedral of Reims in the background.

▲ The *R.E.P.* monoplane made only one flight at Reims. It was named after the initials of its designer, Robert Esnault-Pelterie, a talented engine-builder and pilot.

▼ The *Bleriot XII*, piloted by Bleriot, won a prize for the greatest speed over one lap of the course (10 kilometres).

▼ The *Breguet* biplane made only three brief flights at Reims before it crash-landed and was damaged. It later developed into a famous military aeroplane.

◄ The *Golden Flier*, designed and flown by Glenn Curtiss, was one of the surprises of the Reims meeting. Curtiss won two of the prizes for speed.

► The *Henry Farman III* was designed and flown by Farman, who was undoubtedly the man of the meeting. Farman was a British pilot who spent his whole life in France. After flying Voisin biplanes for many months, Farman designed this magnificent aircraft, which became the most famous European biplane of its time. It was light but strong, with four large and effective ailerons that gave the pilot excellent roll control. Farman won the Reims Grand Prize for the longest flight, over 112 miles, in this machine.

The landing skis were attached to the axle by rubber bands, which would stretch under the shock of landing and allow the skis to skid over rough ground.

◄ The *Antoinette* mono-plane, piloted by Hubert Latham, won the Altitude Prize at Reims for climbing to a height of 508 feet.

▲ The *Voisin* biplane, flown by Etienne Bunau-Varilla, won the Mechanics Prize for flying the longest distance in a fixed time.

These flaps normally hung loose and would adjust themselves to the air streamlines in flight. The pilot lowered them to control turning and balance.

The Reims Meeting

The official title of the Reims airshow was 'The Great Aviation Week of Champagne'. The meeting was initiated, promoted and financed by the champagne industry, which offered generous cash prizes for winners of the events.

The meeting was an unqualified success. Many military and political chiefs attended and were deeply impressed. Most of the aircraft at the Reims meeting were on sale as standard types. The most popular European planes were the *Farmans*, the easy-to-fly *Voisins* and the *Bleriot XI*'s, which had received a great boost in popularity from the Channel crossing.

It was a disappointment that the two first masters of flying – Wilbur and Orville Wright – were too busy in America to attend the Reims meeting. But most of the other great pioneers were present – Farman, Latham, Bleriot, Curtiss and Lefebvre, one of the greatest *Wright A* pilots – and there were many excellent and exciting performances.

There were 38 machines in the final list of entries, but only 23 took off during the eight days, some only briefly. The Grand Prize for distance was won by Farman, who had finished exchanging his Vivinus engine for a rotary Gnome just 40 minutes before the deadline for starting. The 30-kilometre and 20-kilometre speed contests were won by Curtiss with speeds of 46.6 and 47 mph. Bleriot won the 10-kilometre contest at 48 mph. Latham won the Altitude Prize with a climb to 508 feet.

There were some crashes, including the burning of Bleriot's *XII*, but there were no serious injuries. The pilots were troubled by bad weather and gusty winds as well as the general unreliability of their engines.

The Reims meeting led to a great expansion of aircraft and aero-engine design and construction. It also set the fashion for many future airshows in Europe and America. Reims marked the true acceptance of the aeroplane as a practical vehicle.

Appendix 1; 1910-1930

The Early Fighter

▲ 1916. The Morane-Saulnier 'N', known as the Morane *Bullet*, was one of the first fighter aircraft of World War I equipped with a machine gun synchronised to fire through the propeller.

The Biplane Fighter

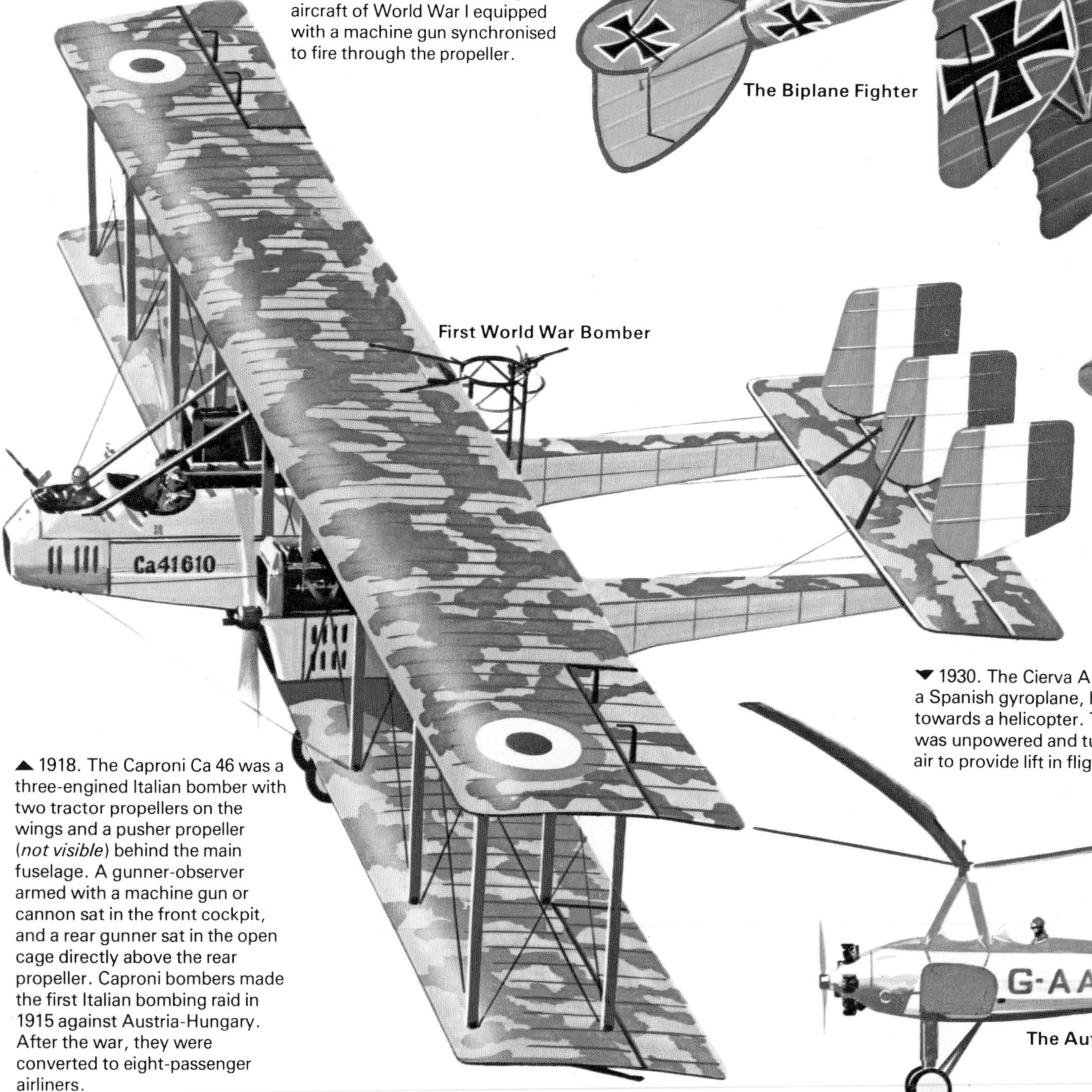

First World War Bomber

▼ 1930. The Cierva Autogiro was a Spanish gyroplane, halfway towards a helicopter. The rotor was unpowered and turned by the air to provide lift in flight.

▲ 1918. The Caproni Ca 46 was a three-engined Italian bomber with two tractor propellers on the wings and a pusher propeller (*not visible*) behind the main fuselage. A gunner-observer armed with a machine gun or cannon sat in the front cockpit, and a rear gunner sat in the open cage directly above the rear propeller. Caproni bombers made the first Italian bombing raid in 1915 against Austria-Hungary. After the war, they were converted to eight-passenger airliners.

The Autogiro

G-AAUA

Ca 41610

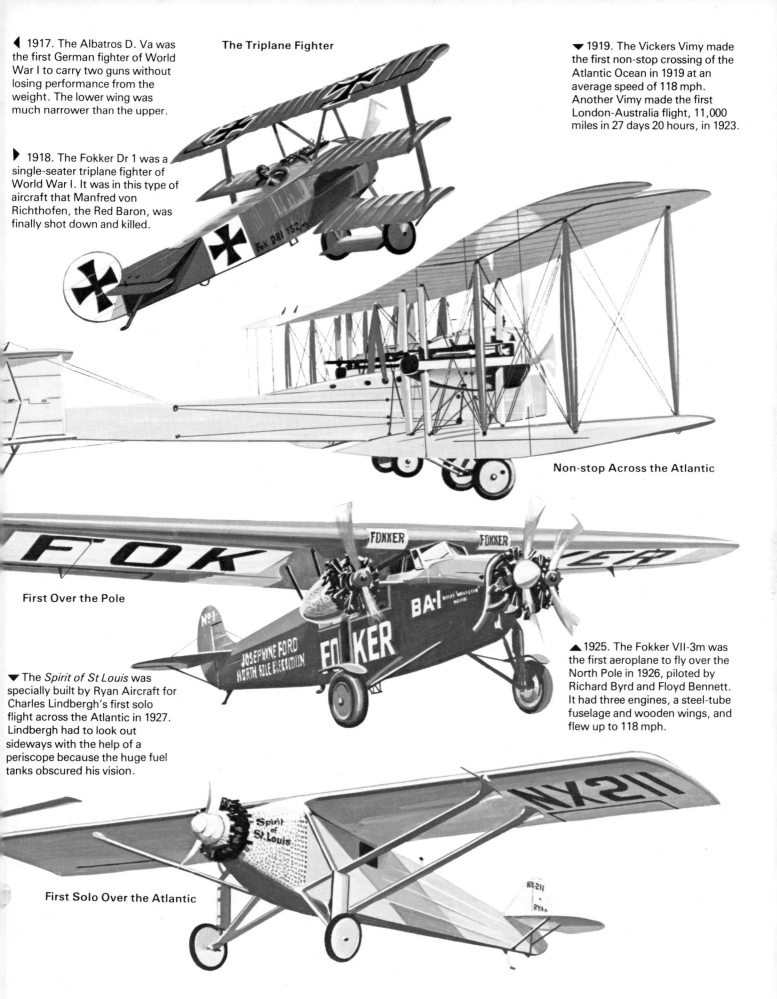

◀ 1917. The Albatros D. Va was the first German fighter of World War I to carry two guns without losing performance from the weight. The lower wing was much narrower than the upper.

The Triplane Fighter

▼ 1919. The Vickers Vimy made the first non-stop crossing of the Atlantic Ocean in 1919 at an average speed of 118 mph. Another Vimy made the first London-Australia flight, 11,000 miles in 27 days 20 hours, in 1923.

▶ 1918. The Fokker Dr 1 was a single-seater triplane fighter of World War I. It was in this type of aircraft that Manfred von Richthofen, the Red Baron, was finally shot down and killed.

Non-stop Across the Atlantic

First Over the Pole

▼ The *Spirit of St Louis* was specially built by Ryan Aircraft for Charles Lindbergh's first solo flight across the Atlantic in 1927. Lindbergh had to look out sideways with the help of a periscope because the huge fuel tanks obscured his vision.

▲ 1925. The Fokker VII-3m was the first aeroplane to fly over the North Pole in 1926, piloted by Richard Byrd and Floyd Bennett. It had three engines, a steel-tube fuselage and wooden wings, and flew up to 118 mph.

First Solo Over the Atlantic

Appendix 2; Then and Now

In under 80 years, the aeroplane has progressed from its first flight to the regular trips of the giant airliner. Flying has become the universal method of transcontinental travel and one of the safest methods of transport ever developed. Modern airliners like the Boeing 747 shown below are capable of carrying nearly 400 passengers at speeds of over 600 mph, altitudes of up to 7 miles, and distances of more than 5,000 miles.

Not only did the first Wright flight lead to the giant airliners of today, but the modest artillery rockets of the 19th Century have resulted in man walking on the moon just 164 years after the rocket was reinvented in Europe.

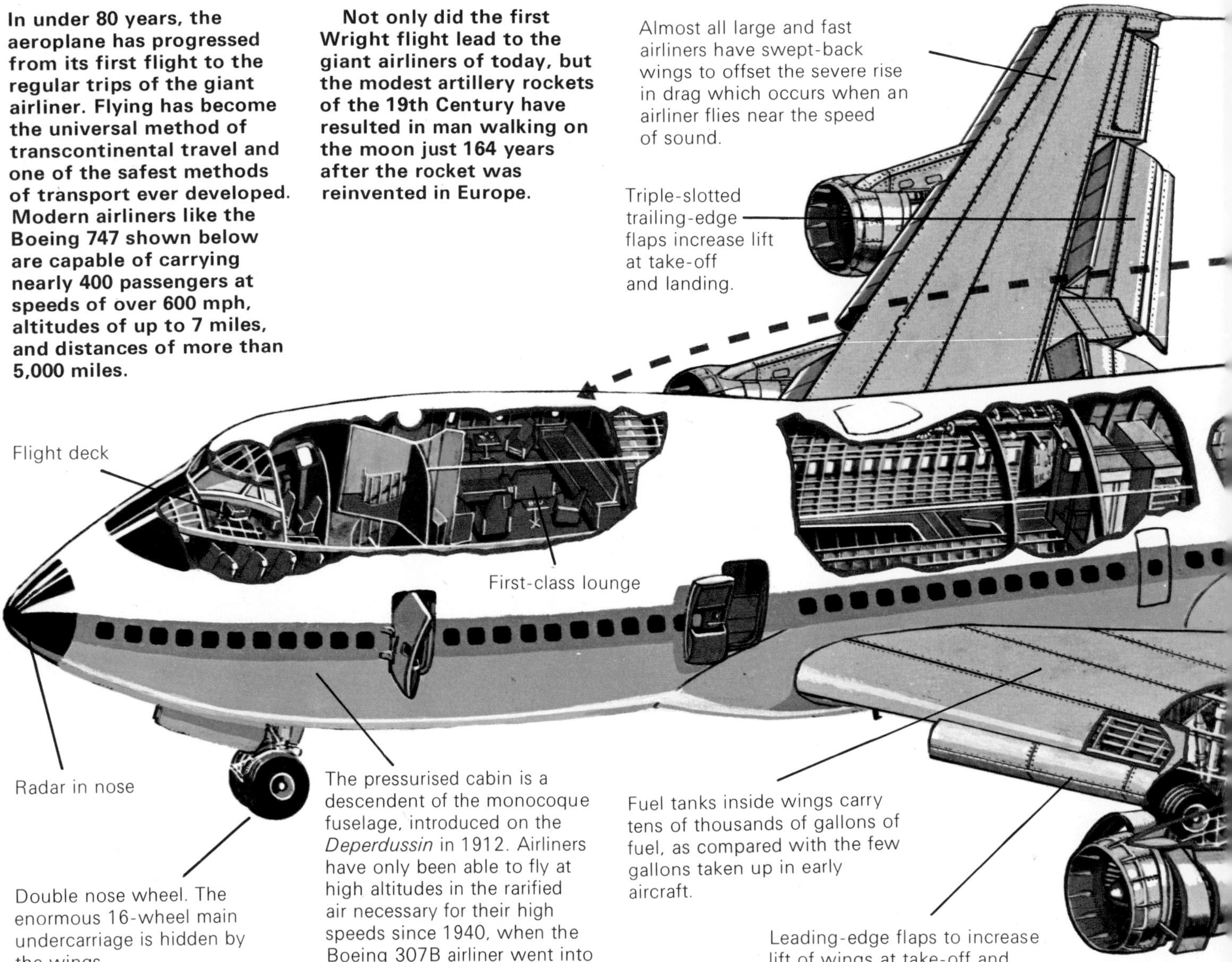

Almost all large and fast airliners have swept-back wings to offset the severe rise in drag which occurs when an airliner flies near the speed of sound.

Triple-slotted trailing-edge flaps increase lift at take-off and landing.

Flight deck

First-class lounge

Radar in nose

Double nose wheel. The enormous 16-wheel main undercarriage is hidden by the wings.

The pressurised cabin is a descendent of the monocoque fuselage, introduced on the *Deperdussin* in 1912. Airliners have only been able to fly at high altitudes in the rarified air necessary for their high speeds since 1940, when the Boeing 307B airliner went into service with the first pressurised cabin.

Fuel tanks inside wings carry tens of thousands of gallons of fuel, as compared with the few gallons taken up in early aircraft.

Leading-edge flaps to increase lift of wings at take-off and landing.

Control systems

▲ The cockpit of Bleriot's *XI* shows the end of the fuel tank and the controls of his monoplane. The 'wheel' is rocked forwards or backwards to control the rear elevator, and sideways to control wing-warping. The levers on the side of the control column are engine controls, and the bar below is operated by foot to control the rudder.

▶ There is nothing radically different in the principles of control used by Bleriot and the Wrights in their day and those used by the pilot of the 747 jumbo jet. The early aviators faced the same problem of controlling their craft in three dimensions as does the modern pilot. The 747 flight deck has over 70 instruments and controls arrayed in front of the pilot and co-pilot.

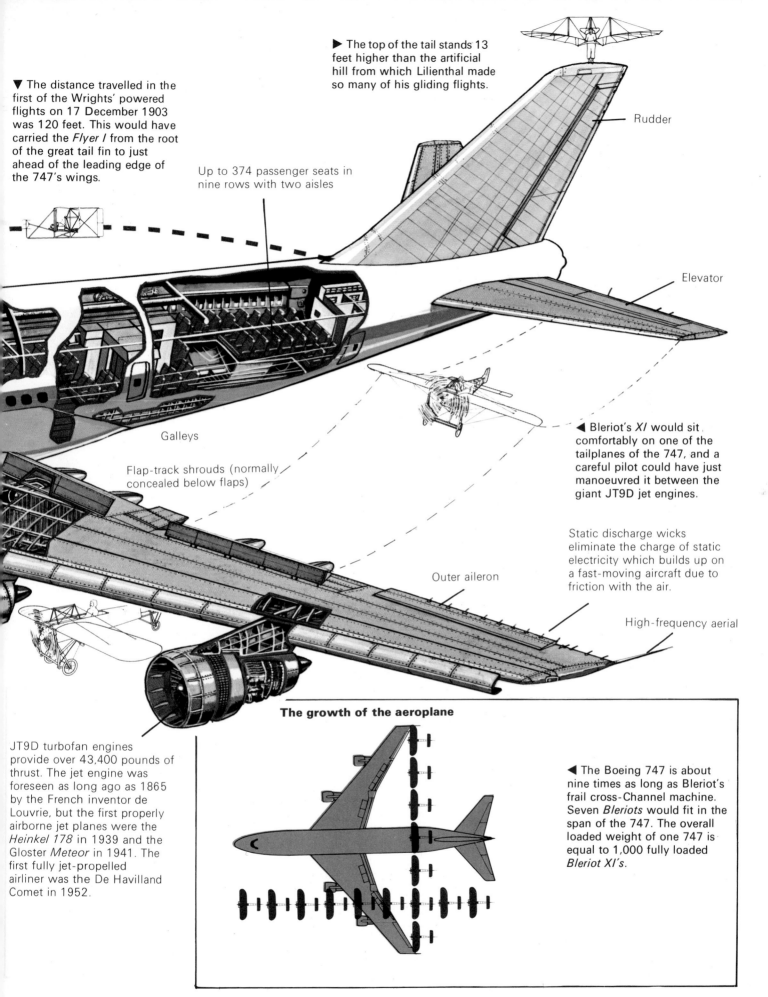

▶ The top of the tail stands 13 feet higher than the artificial hill from which Lilienthal made so many of his gliding flights.

▼ The distance travelled in the first of the Wrights' powered flights on 17 December 1903 was 120 feet. This would have carried the *Flyer I* from the root of the great tail fin to just ahead of the leading edge of the 747's wings.

Up to 374 passenger seats in nine rows with two aisles

Rudder

Elevator

◀ Bleriot's *XI* would sit comfortably on one of the tailplanes of the 747, and a careful pilot could have just manoeuvred it between the giant JT9D jet engines.

Galleys

Flap-track shrouds (normally concealed below flaps)

Static discharge wicks eliminate the charge of static electricity which builds up on a fast-moving aircraft due to friction with the air.

Outer aileron

High-frequency aerial

JT9D turbofan engines provide over 43,400 pounds of thrust. The jet engine was foreseen as long ago as 1865 by the French inventor de Louvrie, but the first properly airborne jet planes were the *Heinkel 178* in 1939 and the Gloster *Meteor* in 1941. The first fully jet-propelled airliner was the De Havilland Comet in 1952.

The growth of the aeroplane

◀ The Boeing 747 is about nine times as long as Bleriot's frail cross-Channel machine. Seven *Bleriots* would fit in the span of the 747. The overall loaded weight of one 747 is equal to 1,000 fully loaded *Bleriot XI's*.

A Time Chart of Aviation 'Firsts'

1783	First aerial voyage by balloon, both hot-air and hydrogen.
1785	First Channel crossing by manned balloon.
1797	First parachute descent from the air, by Garnerin.
1799	First aeroplane design of a modern configuration, incorporating fixed wings, tail-unit control-surfaces and an auxiliary method of propulsion, by Cayley.
1804	First aeroplane model of a modern configuration is flown by Cayley.
1809–1810	Cayley publishes a three-part article which contains the foundations of aerodynamics.
1843	Henson patents his design for an 'Aerial Steam Carriage', a prophetic monoplane design propelled by airscrews.
1847	Henson's model, based on his 1843 design, fails to fly.
1848	Stringfellow's steam-powered model monoplane tested; but it could not sustain itself.
1853	Cayley sends his coachman across a dale in a glider with its controls locked.
1857–1858	First successful powered model aeroplane flight by a clockwork-driven monoplane (Du Temple).
1860	Invention of the gas engine in France, by Lenoir.
1866	Foundation of the Aeronautical Society of Great Britain.
1867	First designs for delta-wing aeroplanes, by Butler and Edwards.
1868	First aeronautical exhibition held — at the Crystal Palace — by the Aeronautical Society.
1868	Stringfellow's steam-powered model triplane tested unsuccessfully; but it was influential, and led to later biplane and triplane production.
1871	Penaud, in France, flies the first inherently stable model aeroplane.
c. 1874	First full-scale man-carrying powered aeroplane takes off but cannot sustain itself (Du Temple).
1876	Invention of the four-stroke petroleum engine by Otto, in Germany.
1884	Phillips takes out patents for double-surface wings, and shows that most of the lift occurs above the wing in an area of low pressure.
1890	First full-scale powered and manned aeroplane takes off under its own power, but cannot fly or be controlled (Ader).
1891	Lilienthal makes his first gliding flights in Germany.
1893	Hargrave invents the box-kite in Australia.
1894	Maxim tests his giant biplane test-rig with small success.
1895–1899	First successful piloted glides in Britain by Pilcher.
1896	Chanute has his influential biplane hang-glider tested successfully.
1896	Lilienthal is killed gliding, and his death sparks great interest in flying.
1896	Motor cars gain the freedom of the roads in Britain, and the resulting growth in mechanical personnel makes ready the necessary technicians for aviation.
1896	Langley has success with his steam-driven model aeroplanes.
1897	Ader twice tests his *Avion III* but it never leaves the ground.
1902	The Wrights perfect their flight-control system on their modified *No. 3* glider.
1902	Ferber builds his first Wright-type glider and has great influence on the Continent.
1903	Langley's full-scale machine twice crashes at take-off.
1903 (Dec 17)	The Wrights make the first powered, sustained, and controlled flights in an aeroplane.
1905	The Wrights' *Flyer III* is the world's first fully practical and successful powered aeroplane.
1906	Santos-Dumont makes the first powered hop-flights in Europe.
1908	The Wrights fly in public and revolutionise world aviation by their mastery of flight control.
1908	First powered flight in Britain by Cody.
1909	Bleriot makes the first aeroplane flight across the English Channel.
1909	The first great aviation meeting is held at Reims, France.
1910	Fabre makes the first seaplane flight.
1919	The first transatlantic flights are made.
1936	The Douglas DC-3 enters service and becomes the most widely used and famous transport in history.
1939	First turbo-jet-propelled aeroplane flies (Heinkel He 178).
1942	The DC-4 first flies and creates a new generation of transports.
1944	First long-range rocket missile becomes operational (German A-4 rocket), which is the beginning of modern space history.
1957	First orbital space craft circles the earth (*Sputnik I*).
1961	First manned spacecraft orbits the earth (Gagarin).
1969	First men to land on the moon (Armstrong and Aldrin).

Index

Numbers in **bold type** refer to illustrations

A-4 rocket, 46
acetylene lamps, Bleriot's, 39
Ader, Clement, 15, 46
Aerial Experimental Association, 36, 37
Aerial Steam Carriage, **10–11**, 11, 30, 46
Aerodrome, 27, **27**, 37
aerodynamics, 6, 9
Aeronautical Society of Great Britain (later Royal Aeronautical Society), 10, 11, 46
ailerons, 30, 31, 37
airliners, 44
airships,
    Cayley's, 8
    de Lana's, 7
    Santos-Dumont's, **29**
Albatross, 12, **13**
Aldrin, B., 46
altitude, 40, 41
Antoinette monoplanes, 30, 43
Antoinette IV, **30–31**, 39, **39**, 41
Antoinette VII, 41, **43**
Antoinette engine, 29, **30**
Anzani engine, 39
Archdeacon, Ernest, 28
Armstrong, N., 46
arrow, 6
artificial hand, invented by Cayley, 9, **10**
Avion III, 46

Baden-Powell, Major B. F. S., 33
Bacqueville, Marquis de, **6**
balloons, **6**, 7, 46
banking, 23, 34
bats, 4, **4**
Bell, Dr Graham, **36**, 37
Bell, Mrs Graham, 37
Berg, Mme Hart O., **33**
Berlin, 16, 17, 37
Besnier, **6**
Bethany, 40
biplanes, 30, 42–43
    Cayley's suggestion for, 9
    Lilienthal gliders, 17, **18–19**
    Maxim's, **14**
    Voisin, 29, 43, **43**
birds, **4–5**
    gliding, 5
    Lilienthal's book on, 17
Blanchard, **6**
Bleriot, Louis, 28, 30, **38–39**, **42**
    Channel flight, 38–39, 46
    on *Wright A.*, 33
    Reims airshow, 41, 42

Bleriot VII, 30, **30**
Bleriot XI, **38–39**, 39, 41, 42, 44, 45
Bleriot XII, 41, 42, **42**
blinkers, **27**
Boeing 307B, 44
Boeing 747, 44, **44–45**
boomerang, 6, **7**
Breguet, Louis, 42
Breguet biplane, 42, **42**
British Government, and Wright brothers, 26
Bunau-Varilla, Etienne, 41, 43
Butler, 46
buzzards, 5, 23

Carillon Park, Dayton, Ohio, 26
catapult launching, 26, 27, 32–33
caterpillar tractor, Cayley's, 9, **10**
Cayley, Sir George, **8**, 30, 46
    analysis of gliding birds, 5, 7
    designs, 8–9
    inventions, 9, **10**
    life, 8
Champagne airshow, 40–43
Channel flight,
    balloon, 46
    Bleriot's, 38–39, 46
Chanute, Octave, 21, 46
Chauvière propeller, **31**, 39
China, 7
Clipper of the Clouds (Verne), 12, 13
Cody, 46
Comet (De Havilland), 45
Congreve, 7
contra-rotation, 12, 25
Cornu, Paul, 28
crashes,
    death of Selfridge, **36**, 37
    Langley's *Aerodrome*, **27**
    Reims airshow, 41
Crystal Palace exhibition, 10, 11, 46
Curtiss, Glenn H., 37, **37**, **42**
    at Reims airshow, 41, 43

Daily Mail, 38, 39
Dandrieux, 12
D'Arlandes, 7
dates of aviation milestones, 46
Dayton, Ohio, 25
De Havilland Comet, 45
De La Landelle, Gabriel, 12
De Lana, 7
De Louvrie, 45
delta-wing designs, 46
Demoiselle, 31
Deperdussin, 44

De Rozier, 7
dimensions of early and modern aircraft, 45
dirigibles, 12
Dollfus, Charles, 39
Douglas DC-3, 46
Douglas DC-4, 46
Dover, 38
Du Temple, Felix, 14–15, 46

Edwards, 46
elevator,
    Cayley's, **8**
    Lilienthal's, 20
    Santos-Dumont's, 29
    use of, in *Wright A.*, **34**
    Wrights', **22**
engine types,
    Antoinette, 29, **30**
    Anzani, 39
    E.N.V., 43
    four-stroke, **15**, 46
    gas, 46
    Gnome, 41, 43
    hot air, 9
    Vivinus, 41
    Wright, **24**, 26
    see also propulsion
E.N.V. engine, 43
Eole, 15, **15**
Escopette (destroyer), 38
Esnault-Pelterie, Robert, **31**, 37, 42, **42**
Europe, flying in, 28–29

Fabre, 46
Farman, Henry, 28, 29, **43**
    at Reims airshow, 40, 41, 43
Farman plane, see *Henry Farman III*
feathers, 4, **4**
Ferber, 46
Five Weeks in a Balloon, 12
flight,
    early attempts, 6–7
    living creatures, 4–5
    powered, 6, 15, 24–25
flight control,
    ailerons vs. wing-warping, 30, 31, 37
    birds, 5
    Bleriot XI, **44**
    Boeing 747, **44–45**
    Cayley's designs, 8–9
    development of on gliders, 6
    movable surfaces for, 21
    progress in, by Wright brothers, 22–23, **27**, 33
    shifting of pilot's weight, **16–17**, **18**, **19**, 21, 23
    Wright A., **34**

Fontana, 7
Forlanini, Enrico, 12
Fort Myer, 36, 37
France,
    flying in, 28
    Wright brothers in, 26, 32, 33

Gagarin, Yuri, 46
gannet, **4–5**
Garnerin, **7**, 46
Gastambide-Mengin I, 30, **30**
gliders,
    Cayley's design for, **9**
    Cayley's model, 10
    float-gliders, Voisin's, 21, 28, **28**, 39
    hang-glider, Chanute's, **21**
    Lilienthal's, **16**, **18–19**, 20
    Pilcher's *Hawk*, **20–21**
    Wright brothers', **22–23**, 23
gliding,
    birds, 5
    first development of flight control in, 5, 6, 15, 23, 28
Gloster *Meteor*, 45
Gnome engine, 41, 43
Golden Flier, 37, **40–41**, **42**, 43
Gollenberg, 20
Gordon Bennett trophy, 40–41

Hargrave, Lawrence, 21, 46
Harpon (destroyer), 39
Hawk, **20–21**
Heinkel 178, 45
helicopters,
    Cornu's, **28**
    hummingbird, 4, **5**
    models, **6**, 8, **9**, 12
    19th c. craze for, 12
Henry Farman III, **40–41**, 43, **43**
Henson, William, 11, 30, 46
hop-flights, 28, 29, 46
Huffman Prairie, Ohio, 25, 26
hummingbird, 4, **5**
Hunaudieres racecourse, 32

jet engines, 45, 46
JT9D turbofan engines, 45
June Bug, 37, **37**

Kill Devil Hills, Kitty Hawk, 24, 25
kites, 6, **7**
    box-kite, 21, **21**
Kitty Hawk, N. Carolina, 23, 24

landing,
    Lilienthal glider, **16**, **17**, **18**, **19**
    Wright A., 33, **35**
Langley, Samuel Pierpont, 27, 37, 46